- 20 Reproducible Bible Memory Verse Coloring Posters
- 6 Reproducible Student Awards and Certificates
- 40 Craft Projects for Children
- 10 Craft Projects for Youth

Compiled by Neva Hickerson and Christy Weir

The patterns in this book may be reproduced.

© Copyright 1990 by Gospel Light Publications,
Ventura, California 93006. All rights reserved.

Printed in U.S.A.
Library of Congress Cataloging in Publication Data

Hickerson, Neva.
    Treasure chest of crafts : 20 reproducible Bible memory verse coloring posters, 6 reproducible student awards and certificates, 40 crafts projects for children, 10 craft projects for youth / compiled by Neva Hickerson and Christy Weir.
    p.   cm.
    ISBN 0-8307-1348-4
    1. Bible crafts. I. Weir, Christy. II. Title.
BS613.H53   1990
268′.432—dc20

89-23690
CIP

Scripture quotations are from the *Holy Bible, New International Version*. Copyright © 1973, 1978, 1984 International Bible Society. Used by permission of Zondervan Bible Publishers.

Contents

Crafts Can Teach 5
Stimulating Bible Learning Through Crafts 6
Preparing to Do Crafts 7
List of Materials 8
Helpful Hints 9

SECTION 1 Crafts for Young Children 11

Beach in a Jar   12
Happy Healed Man   13
Spool Animal   14
Helping Hands   16
Finger Friends   16
Church Mouse   17
Stand-Up Tree   18
Flip-Flop Face   20
Stitch Card   21
Wonder Window   22

SECTION 2 Crafts for Younger Elementary 23

Sand Painting   24
Good Samaritan Doll   25
Butterfly   26
Kindness Kritter Pencil   27
Thumbprint Creature   28
Daisy Flower   28
Love Stencil Poster   29
Hymnbook   32
Hanging Holder   33
Angel Bookmark   34

SECTION 3 Crafts for Older Elementary 35

Island in the Son Plaque   36
Goofy Glasses   37
Happy Man Mobile   38
Kindness Cookie Tub   40
Wooden Key Holder   41
Gift Potpourri Pouch   42
Bread Dough Napkin Rings   43
Doorknob Hanger   44
Swirl Banner   45
Sonrise Flower Pot   45
Plaster Plaque   46
Tropical Fish Yarn Design   47
Mirror Ink Prints   48
Underwater Mobile   48
Seaside Bath Delight   50
Huggy Panda Pencil   51
Linoleum Mosaic   51
Bird Feeder   52
Wire Bracelet   53
Trefoil   54

SECTION 4 Crafts for Youth 55

Cigar Box Collage   56
Landscape in a Basket   56
"Stone" Carving   57
Seashell Picture Frame   58
Decorative Wire Basket   59
Tropical Fruit Magnets   59
Shell Comb   60
Personal Chalkboard   60
Friendship Bracelet   61
Rainbow Jar   62

SECTION 5 Reproducible Pages 63

Bible Memory Verse Coloring Pages
For Younger Elementary
For Older Elementary

Certificates and Awards

Index 113

Crafts Can Teach

"Crafts are for . . .
 . . . keeping kids busy!
  . . . giving them something to take home.
   . . . using up a lot of throw-away materials.
    . . . helping children learn."

While all of the above are true to a point, the last statement is the focus of this article.

Crafts can be a means of helping children learn many things, such as:

"Mandy doesn't like having her face spattered with paint."
 "Fake fur tickles!"
  "Three out of four of our glue bottles are clogged."
   "Not all marking pens wash off."
    "Ramon won't share the scissors!"
Useful information like that.

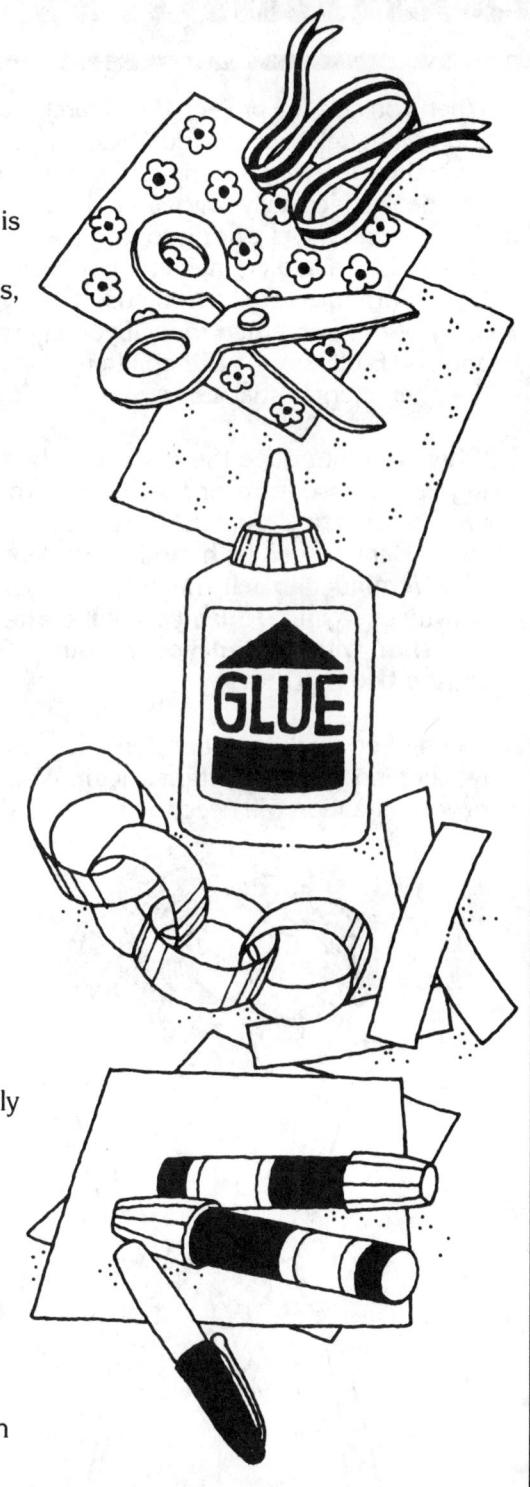

And more besides. Some people use craft projects to help children learn about—

- finishing what they start
- developing their artistic capacities
- working well with others
- using materials wisely
- handling satisfaction over a good achievement
- handling frustration over a "failed" project.

Children do need to learn those things.

But crafts can also help reinforce Bible learning, by giving a child something physical to do as an expression of something heard in a Bible story.

And the Bible verse depicted on a craft project can repeatedly bring those important words back to a child's thinking.

Such learning is important and is the main reason for this book. You'll find a wide variety of project ideas to use with children from age three through fourteen.

And most of them are easily adaptable to help you reinforce whatever Bible lesson you want to be sure is not forgotten.

Turn the page to see some examples of how crafts really can support Bible learning.

Stimulating Bible Learning Through Crafts

1. When you select a project, think carefully of how you might relate it to your teaching purpose. Even though every description in this book may not deal specifically with your lesson, a little thought can usually bring to mind several ideas of how to make a connection. For example, the Good Samaritan Doll can be used to review the story of the Samaritan man. If you are teaching another Bible story, have children make one of the characters in that story.

2. When you introduce the craft, start by explaining its purpose in regard to Bible learning, not just its practical function. For example, the "Swirl Banner" can be hung in a student's room as a reminder to tell the truth. Introduce the activity by saying, **Today you will make a banner that will remind you to obey God by telling the truth.**

3. As children work, be conscious of your role as teacher, not just as craft instructor. While much of your attention will need to be given to helping children complete the project successfully, look for moments to slip in a question about the craft's teaching purpose. All of the craft projects in this book have "Conversation Suggestions" to help stimulate your thinking of appropriate questions to ask or comments to offer.

4. Pay attention to the interaction among children as well as the work they are doing. A lesson about bragging can be put to the test as children notice each other's work. Or a lesson on forgiveness can be illustrated when a child forgives a friend for bumping his or her arm.

5. As work is concluding, ask children to tell how their project relates to that day's Bible learning. Ask questions such as: **What will this help you remember about (Jesus' care)? How can you use this to show that you have learned about (Jesus' care)? What could you say about this craft to (a friend, your parents, etc.) that would help explain what you've learned?**

Preparing to Do Crafts

- **If you are planning to use crafts with a child at home, here are three helpful tips:**

1. Focus on the projects in the section for your child's age, but don't ignore projects that are listed for older or younger ages. Elementary aged children enjoy many of the projects grouped under "Crafts for Young Children" and they can do them with little or no adult assistance. And younger children are always interested in doing "big kid" things. Just plan on working along with the child, helping with tasks the child cannot handle alone.

2. Start with projects which call for materials you have around the house. Make a list of items you do not have which are needed for projects you think your child will enjoy. Plan to gather those supplies in one expedition.

3. If certain materials seem too difficult to obtain, a little thought can usually lead to appropriate substitutions. And often the homemade version ends up being a real improvement over the original plan.

- **If you are planning to lead a group of children in doing craft projects, keep these hints in mind:**

1. Choose projects which will allow children to work with a variety of materials.

2. Make your selection of all projects far enough in advance of need to allow time to gather all needed supplies in one coordinated effort. Many projects use some of the same items.

3. Make up a sample of each project to be sure the directions are fully understood and potential problems can be avoided. You may find you will want to adapt some projects to simplify procedures or vary the materials required.

4. Many items can be acquired as donations from people or businesses if you plan ahead and make your needs known. Many churches distribute lists of materials needed to their congregation and community and are able to provide crafts at little or no cost. Some items can be brought by the children themselves (e.g., plastic detergent bottles for "Good Samaritan Doll" or juice cans for "Kindness Kritter Pencil Holders").

5. In making your supplies list, distinguish between items which every individual child will need and those which will be shared among a group.

6. Keep in mind that some materials may be shared among more than one age level, but only if there is good coordination among the groups. It is extremely frustrating to a teacher to expect to have scissors, only to discover another group is using them. Basic supplies which are used repeatedly in craft projects should usually be provided to every group.

7

List of Materials

Since you will probably never try to do all the projects described in this book, we did not attempt to list every item needed. The "Basic Supplies" section indicates supplies used repeatedly in a large number of the projects. The "Specialized Materials" section is intended to call attention to items which are used frequently but might require special effort to secure.

NOTE: A complete list of materials needed for each craft is found in the directions for that specific craft project.

Basic Supplies

For Young Children

Containers—shallow pie tins
              plastic margarine tubs
Glue—white
      tacky
Hole punch
Markers—crayons
        felt pens
        fine-tip permanent
        pencils
Paint—liquid tempera
      watercolor
Paintbrushes (wide bristle)
Paper—construction
       butcher or shelf
Paper clips
String
Tape—masking
      transparent
Yarn

For Elementary Children and Youth

Add to list for Young Children:
Chalk/chalkboard
Hot glue gun and glue sticks
Iron/Ironing board
Paint—poster
      acrylic
Paintbrushes (fine tip)
Paper—8½ × 11-inch white
Ruler

For Clean Up

Detergent
Dishpan (if water is not available in room)
Newspapers
Paper towels
Plastic drop cloth
Smocks (aprons, old shirts, etc.)
Sponges

Specialized Materials

Chenille wire
Clothespins
Craft knife
Craft Sticks
Fishing line
Felt (various colors)
Food—dry beans
      salad macaroni
Paper—waxed
      clear, adhesive-backed
      tracing
Paper plates
Pom-poms (variety of sizes and colors)
Trim material—ribbon
        lace
        rickrack
Wiggle eyes (variety of sizes)

Helpful Hints

Using Glue with Young Children

Since preschoolers have difficulty using glue bottles effectively, you may want to try one of the following procedures. Purchase glue in large containers (up to one gallon size).

a. Pour small amount of glue into several shallow containers.

b. Dilute glue by mixing a little water into each container.

c. Children use paste brushes to spread glue on project.

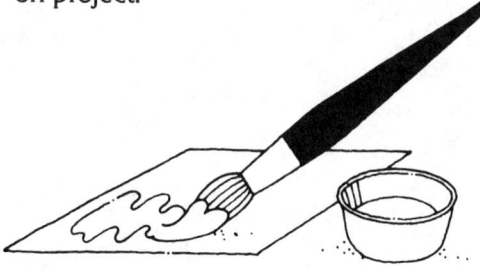

OR

a. Pour a small amount of glue into a plastic margarine tub.

b. Give each child a cotton swab. The child dips the cotton swab into the glue and rubs glue on project.

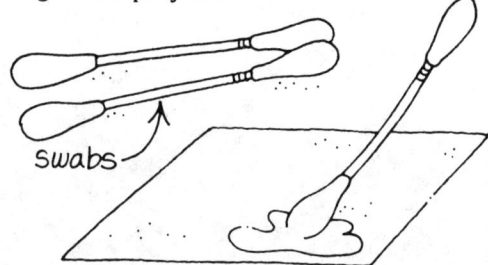

c. Excess glue can be poured back into the large container at the end of each session.

How to Make Patterns

You will need: Tissue paper, lightweight cardboard, pencil, scissors.

a. Trace pattern from book onto tissue paper.

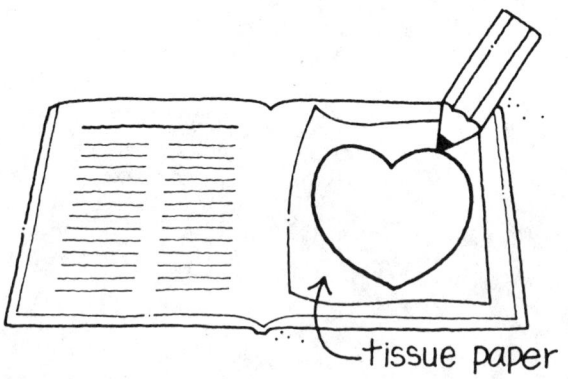

b. Cut out tissue paper pattern and trace onto cardboard.

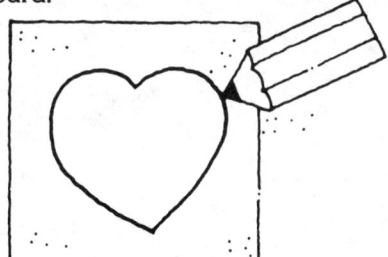

c. Cut out cardboard pattern.

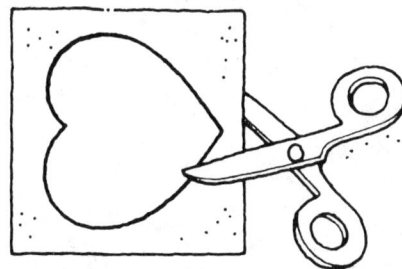

Cutting with Scissors

When cutting with scissors is required for these crafts, take note of the fact that some of the children in your class may be left-handed. It is very difficult for a left-handed person to cut with scissors that were designed to be used with the right hand. Have available in your classroom two or three pairs of left-handed scissors. These can be obtained from a school supply center.

SECTION 1/AGES 2-5

Crafts for Young Children

Craft projects for young children are a blend of, "I wanna do it myself!" and "I need help!" Each project, because it is intended to come out looking like a recognizable something, usually requires a certain amount of adult assistance—in preparing a pattern, in doing some cutting, in preselecting magazine pictures, in using the iron, etc.

The younger the child, the more the adult will need to do, but care must always be taken not to rob the child of the satisfaction of his or her own unique efforts. Neither must the adult's desire to have a nice finished project override the child's pleasure at experimenting with color and texture. Avoid the temptation to do the project for the child or to improve on the child's efforts.

Some of the crafts have enrichment and simplification ideas included with them. An enrichment idea provides a way to make the craft more challenging for the older child. A simplification idea helps the younger child complete the craft more successfully.

If you find a child frustrated with some of the limitations of working on a structured craft—although most of the projects in this book allow plenty of leeway for children to be themselves—it may be a signal that child needs the opportunity to work on more creative, less structured materials: blank paper and paints, play dough, or abstract collages (gluing miscellaneous shapes or objects onto surfaces such as paper, cardboard or anything else to which glue will adhere). Remember the cardinal rule of thumb in any task a young child undertakes: the process the child goes through is more important than the finished product.

Beach in a Jar

Materials: Sand in a variety of colors (available in craft supply stores), large open containers, plastic spoons, paper clips, fabric and felt scraps, scissors, glue. For each child—baby food jar with lid. Optional—(materials for making your own colored sand) water, fine sand, powdered fabric dyes, containers in which to dye sand, paper towels, newspapers.

Preparation: Pour colored sand into large open containers (so children have easy access to sand). Cut 5-inch (12.5-cm) circles from fabric, one for each child. Cut 15-inch (37.5-cm) lengths of yarn, one for each child. Provide each child with several paper cups, a spoon and a baby food jar.

Optional—(to dye sand) fill containers one-half to two-thirds full of sand—one container for each color of powdered fabric dye. Add enough water to cover sand completely. Add a spoonful of powdered fabric dye. Stir and let sit for fifteen minutes. Then carefully pour out as much water as possible without losing the sand. Spoon sand onto newspaper pads covered with paper toweling and spread to dry for 12-24 hours.

Instruct each child in the following procedures:

- Carefully spoon layers of colored sand (alternating colors for each layer) on top of each other into jar. The last layer should come just to neck of jar.
- Open a paper clip into a straight piece of wire. Push wire down through all the layers of sand, keeping wire against glass. This will make a design in the sand which can be seen through jar. (Younger children will need teacher assistance.) Then remove wire (sketch a).
- Make these designs with wire all the way around jar.
- When design is finished, fill jar all the way to the top with sand and screw on lid securely.
- Child holds fabric circle on lid while teacher ties with yarn (sketch b).

Enrichment Idea: Older children might enjoy decorating top of lid by gluing small shells or beads to fabric.

Conversation Suggestions: Affirm children who voluntarily share and are kind to each other. **Kari, making room for Joshua at the sand table was a kind thing to do. We can show we love others by being kind to each other. What are some ways God shows He loves us? One of the ways God showed He loves us was by sending His Son, Jesus.**

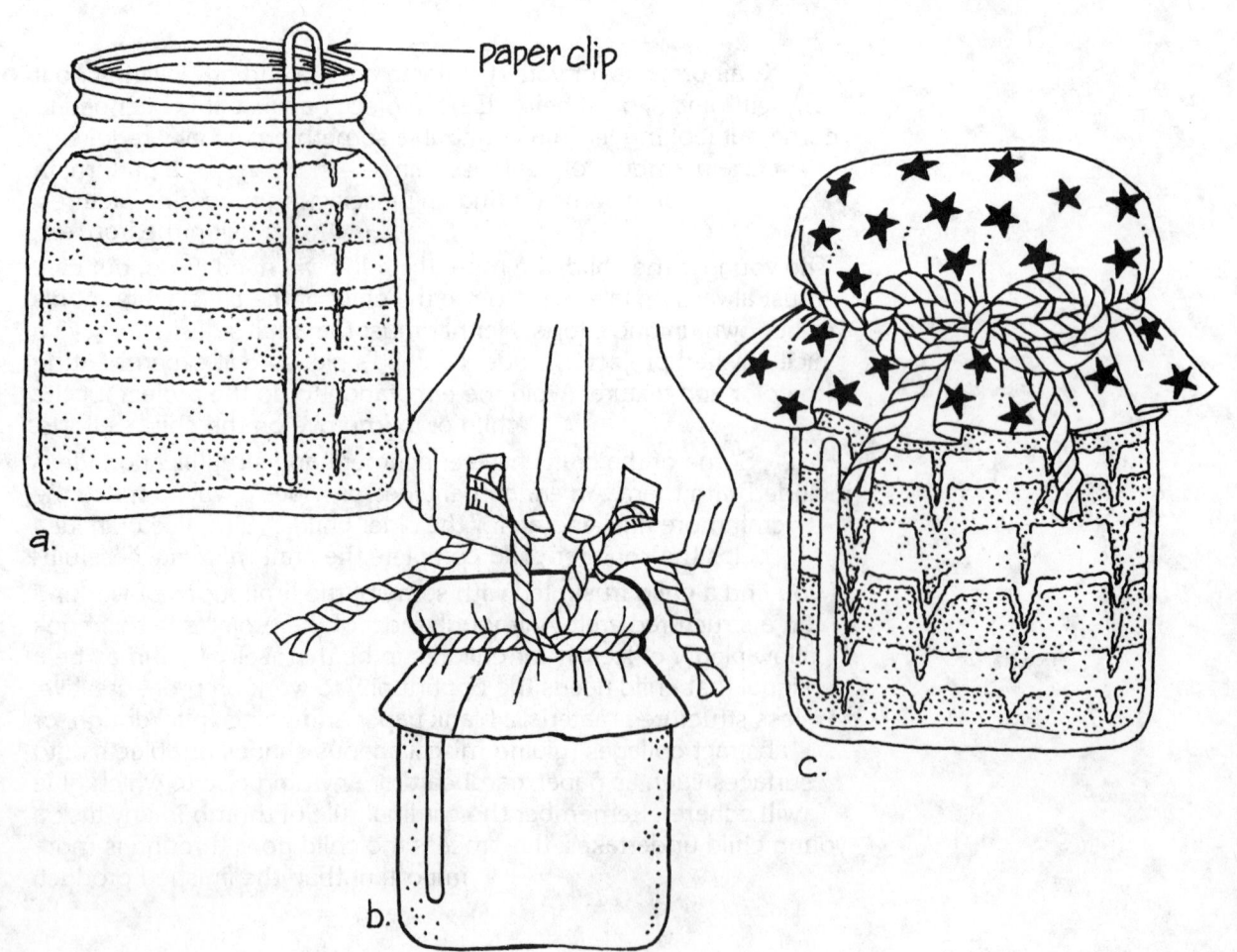

Happy Healed Man

Materials: Body, Feet and Hand Patterns, large rubber bands, staples, staplers, crayons, scissors, yarn, hole punch, construction paper, photocopy machine.

Preparation: Photocopy Body, Feet and Hand Patterns onto construction paper—one set for each child. Cut yarn into 6-inch (15-cm) lengths—one for each child.

Instruct each child in the following procedures:
- Use crayons to color face and clothes.
- Use scissors to cut out Happy Man's body, feet and hands.
- Use scissors to cut four rubber bands.
- With teacher's help, staple a rubber band to each hand and foot (sketch a). Then staple opposite end of each rubber band to appropriate part of body.
- Use hole punch to punch hole in head.
- Thread yarn through hole and tie in loop.

Enrichment Idea: Children glue yarn pieces to head for hair.

Conversation Suggestions: **Who did Jesus help in our Bible story? Why do you think Jesus helped? Can you make your healed man jump with joy?**

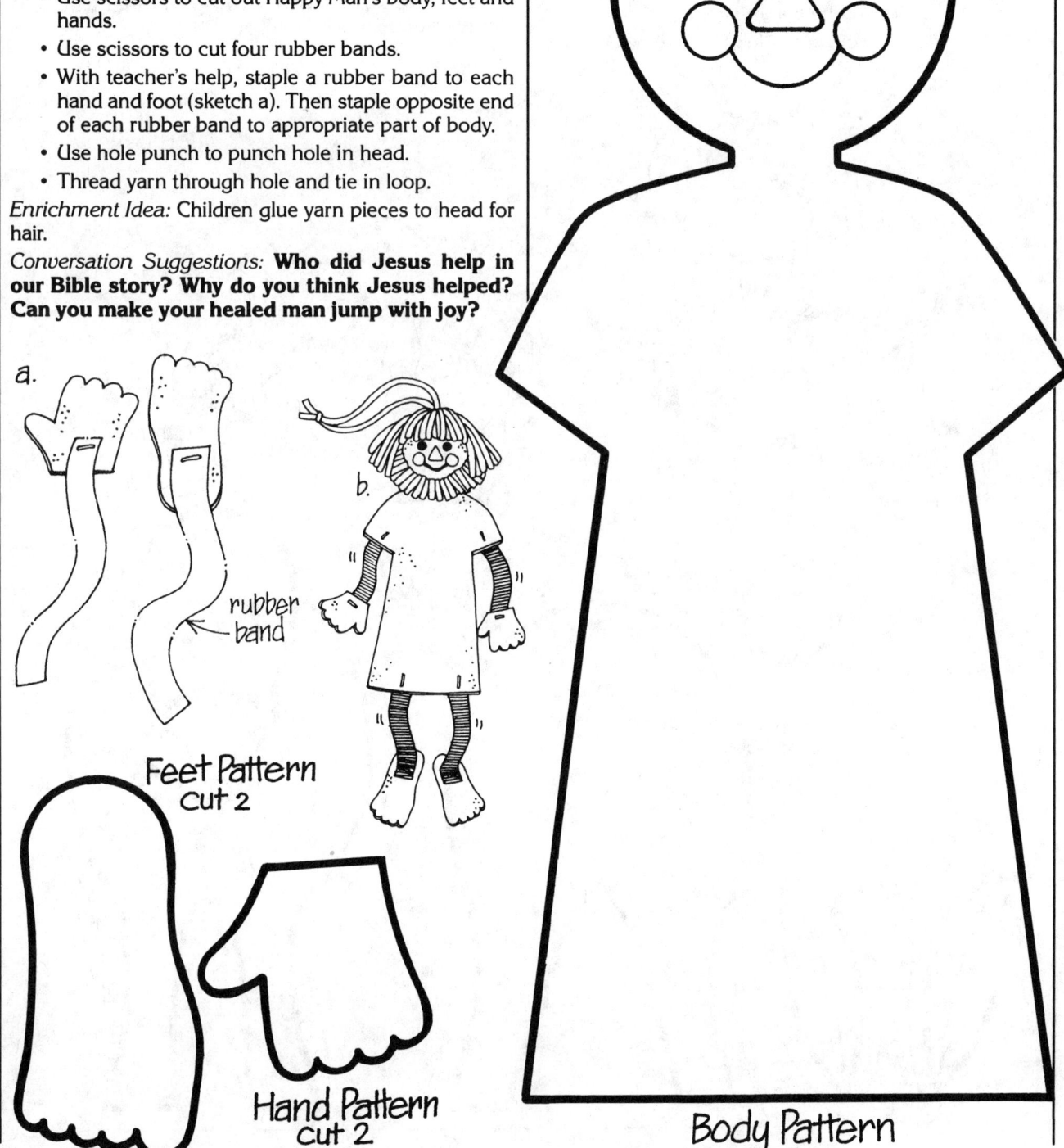

Spool Animal

Materials: Spool Animal Patterns (including ear patterns), spools (or tissue rolls cut in two), construction paper, glue, scissors, cotton balls for sheep, yarn and photocopy machine. Optional—scraps of black, pink and brown felt, wiggle eyes.

Preparation: Choose an animal related to the lesson for each child to make. Photocopy Animal Pattern onto construction paper—one for each child. Cut yarn into 2-inch (5-cm) lengths for Donkey, Cow or Pig tails.

Instruct each child in the following procedures:
- Use scissors to cut out Animal Pattern pieces.
- Glue yarn or cotton ball to back piece for tail.
- Glue ears to animal's head. Let dry.
- Glue front and back body pieces to spool (sketch a). For lamb, glue cotton balls to spool (sketch b).

Enrichment Idea: Children glue felt ears (cut out by teacher) and wiggle eyes to animal.

Conversation Suggestions: **What kind of animal did you make? What kind of animal did we hear about in our Bible story? When you go home, who will you tell about our Bible story?**

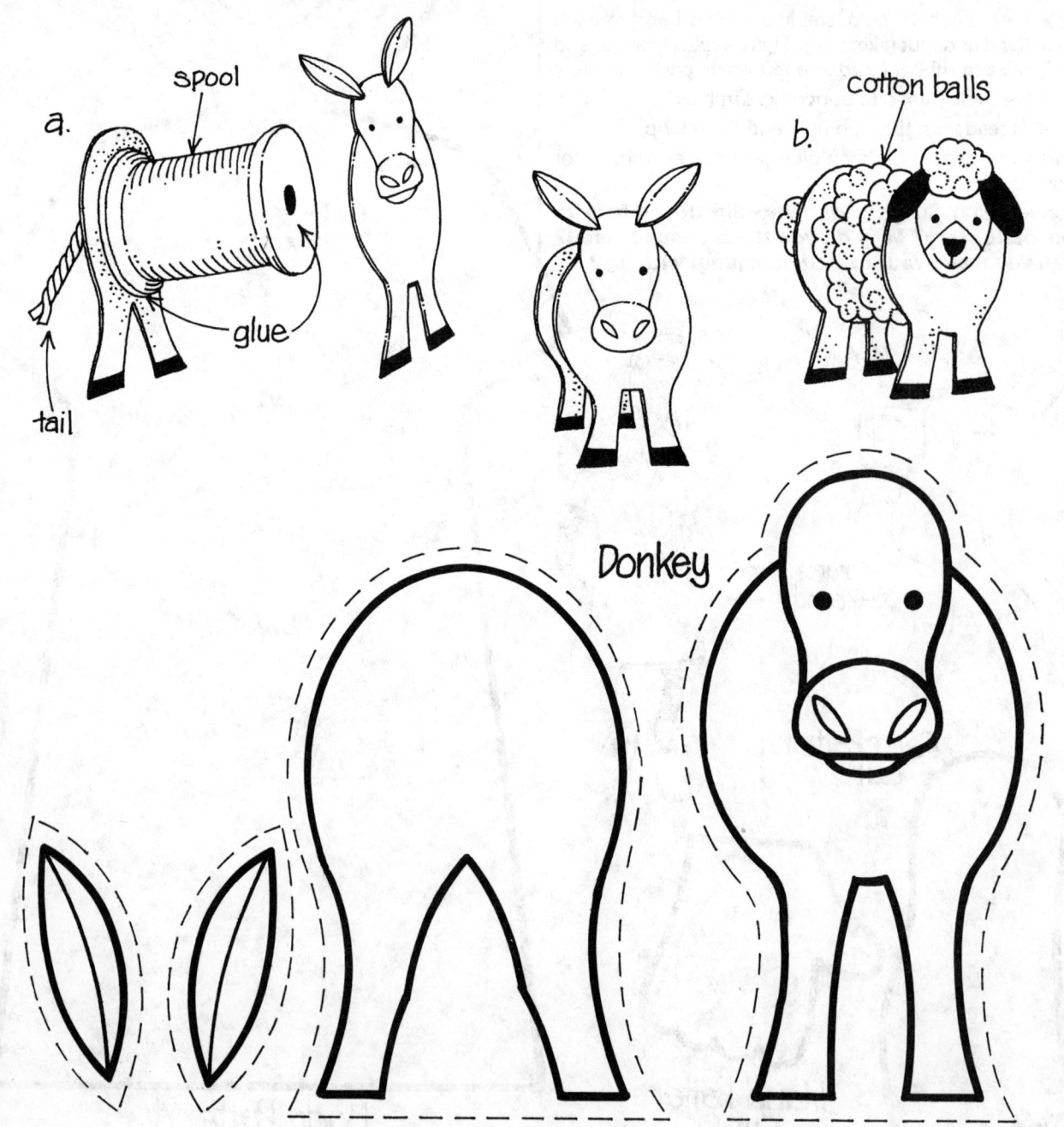

14

Spool Animal Patterns

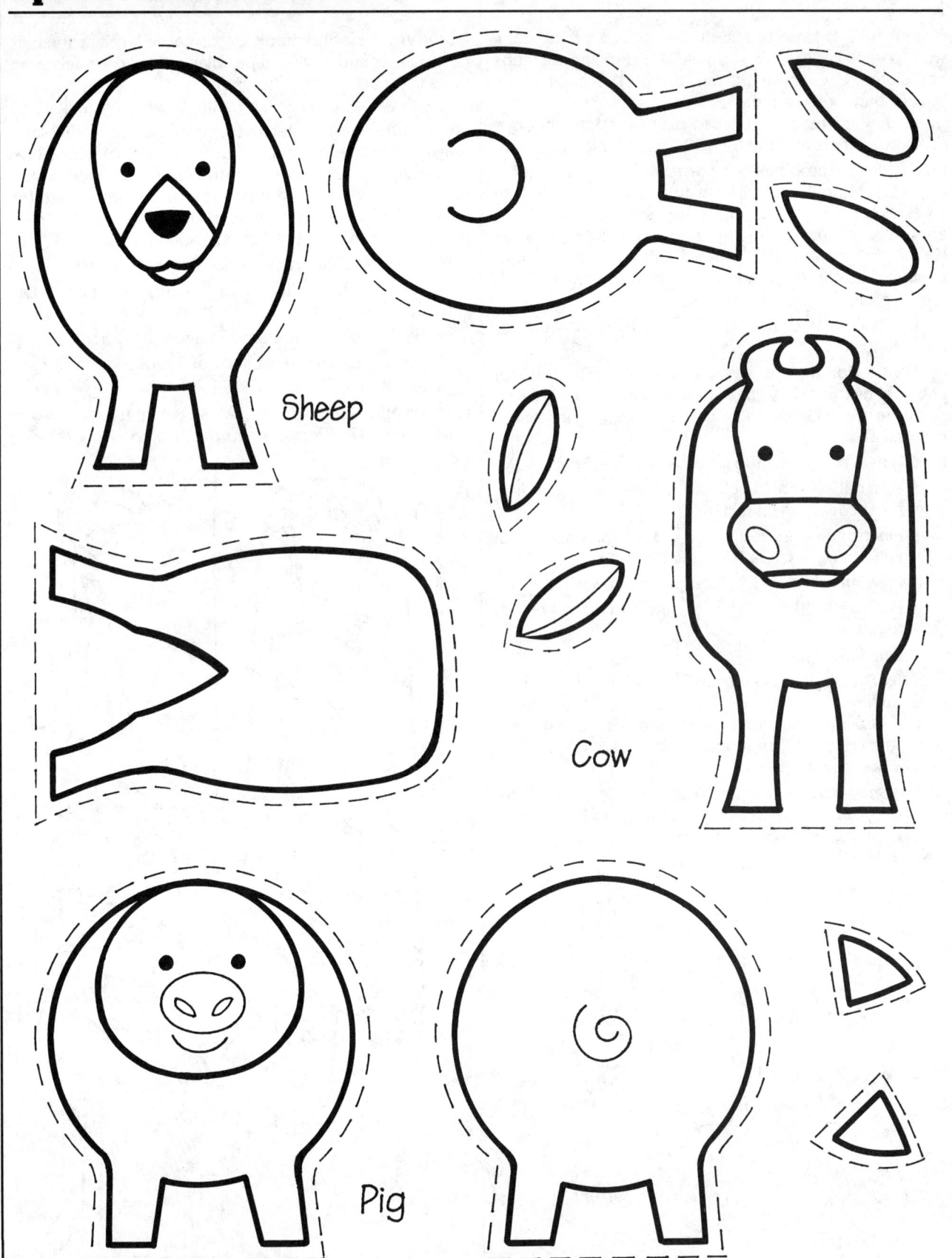

Helping Hands

Materials: Two large bowls, one small bowl, flour sifter, wooden spoon, 4 cups flour (NOT self-rising), 2 cups cornstarch, 2 cups salt, 2 tsp. glycerin, 2 cups water, plastic bag, rolling pins, cookie sheets, sealer spray, oven, dull knives, pencil, salad plates, ribbon, scissors. (This quantity is enough for six to eight children.)

Preparation: Combine flour, cornstarch and salt in large bowl. Stir ingredients. Sift mixture into large bowl. In small bowl mix glycerin and water, stirring well. Slowly add water mixture to dry ingredients, stirring constantly. Knead dough until stiff and smooth—about five minutes. Put dough in plastic bag and store overnight in refrigerator.

Cut ribbon into 12-inch (30-cm) lengths—one for each child.

Divide dough into baseball-sized lumps—one for each child. You may want to provide an additional lump of clay for each child to play with while waiting for teacher's assistance.

Instruct each child in the following procedures:
- Use rolling pin to roll out dough to ¼-inch (.6-mm) thickness (sketch a).
- Place plate over dough and cut around dough with knife to form circle (sketch b).
- Press hand firmly into dough (sketch c).
- Push pencil through top of plaque to make hole for hanging.
- Place plaque on cookie sheet.

Teacher then bakes plaques in 275 degrees Fahrenheit (135 degrees Celsius) oven for one hour. Turn oven off and allow plaques to cool in oven for at least one hour to eliminate cracking. Spray with sealer. Let dry. Insert ribbon in hole and tie.

Conversation Suggestions: **What are some ways you can use your hands to help others?** (Picking up toys, giving a hug.) **How can you help someone in our class today?**

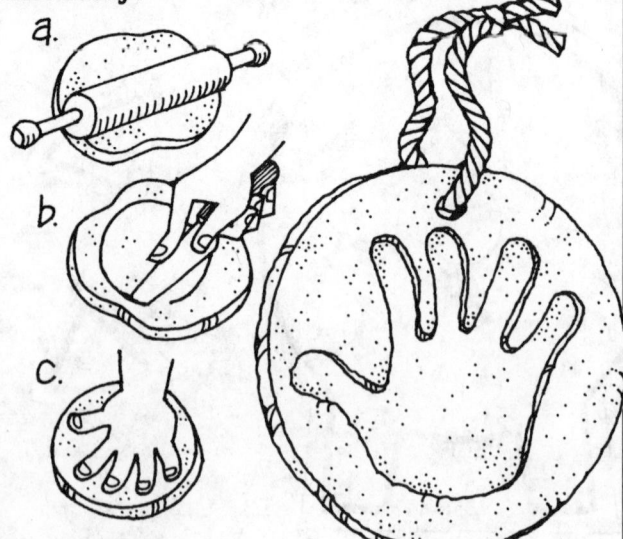

Finger Friends

Materials: Coloring book or discarded magazines or catalogs, chenille wire, tape, black crayon or felt pen, scissors, glue, construction paper.

Preparation: For each child—choose one 3-inch (7.5-cm) figure (without legs) from magazine. Use black crayon or felt pen to outline figure to make a cutting line for children (sketch a). Cut around each outlined figure. Cut chenille wire into 6-inch (15-cm) lengths—one for each child. Twist each wire as in sketch b. Cut construction paper into 5-inch (12.5-cm) squares.

Instruct each child in the following procedures:
- Glue magazine figure to construction paper. Let dry.
- Use scissors to cut around figure on black line.
- Tape chenille wire to back of figure (sketch c).
- Use figure as a finger puppet.

Conversation Suggestions: **What is the name of your finger friend? What can (name) do to show love?**

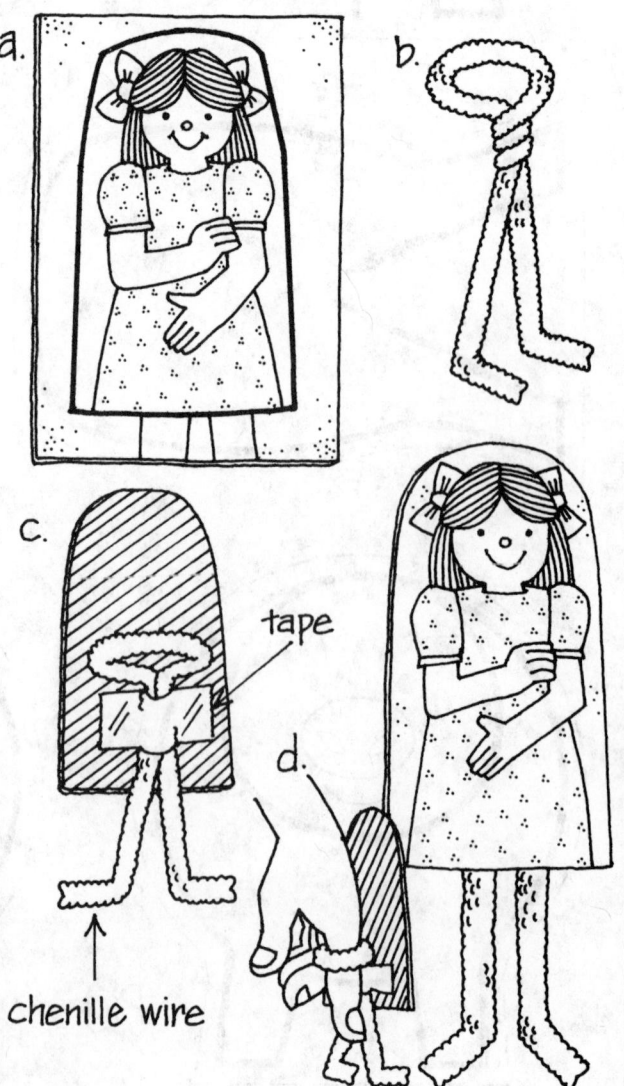

Church Mouse

Materials: Mouse Body, Head and Ear Patterns, pencil, scissors, gray and pink felt, gray yarn, glue, black felt pen, cardboard.

Preparation: Trace patterns onto cardboard and cut out. (See "How to Make Patterns," p. 9.) Trace around cardboard patterns onto felt. Cut body and head from gray felt. Cut two ears from pink felt. Make one set for each child. Cut yarn into 9-inch (22.5-cm) lengths—one for each child.

Instruct each child in the following procedures:

- Glue yarn to body for tail.
- Glue head to body.
- Glue ears to head.
- Use black felt pen to draw eyes and nose.

Conversation Suggestion: **How would you feel if someone said, "My mouse is better than yours. Ha, ha, ha!"** (Sad or angry.) **What is a kind thing you might say while we are making our bookmarks?** ("Kenny, I like the way you made your mouse!" or "LaShonda, would you like to share my glue?")

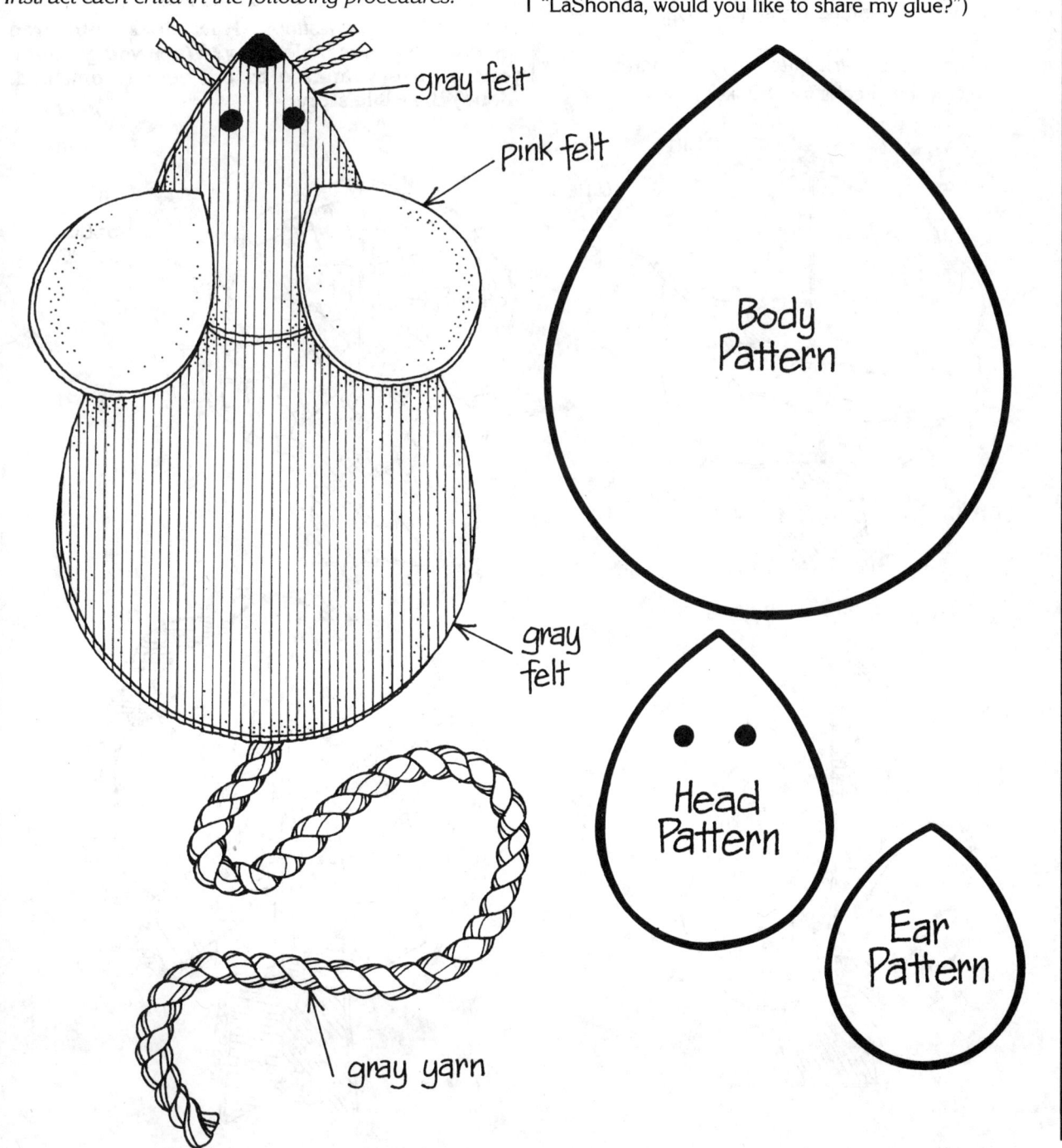

Stand-up Tree

Materials: Stand-up Tree Pattern, lightweight cardboard, green, yellow, red and orange tissue paper, pencil, glue, water, shallow pans, glue brushes, scissors, brown crayons.

Preparation: Trace pattern onto cardboard and cut out. (See "How to Make Patterns," p. 9.) Then trace cardboard pattern onto cardboard and cut out—two for each child. Cut slit on one tree piece from top to middle and cut slit on other tree piece from bottom to middle as indicated on pattern. Cut or tear tissue paper into 2-inch (5-cm) squares. Pour glue into shallow pans. Dilute glue with water.

Instruct each child in the following procedures:
- Use crayons to color tree trunks.
- Brush a small amount of glue on tree (sketch a). Press several pieces of tissue onto glue.
- Repeat process until trees are covered with tissue (sketch b). Brush over tissue paper with a layer of glue. (Make sure slits in trees are not covered with tissue.)
- With teacher's help, slide one tree piece onto the slit of other tree piece (sketch c) and stand tree up.

Simplification Idea: Younger children may crumple tissue, then press onto glue and onto tree.

Conversation Suggestions: **How does your tree remind you of our Bible story? When you go home you can use your tree to tell your (mom, dad, friend) the Bible story.**

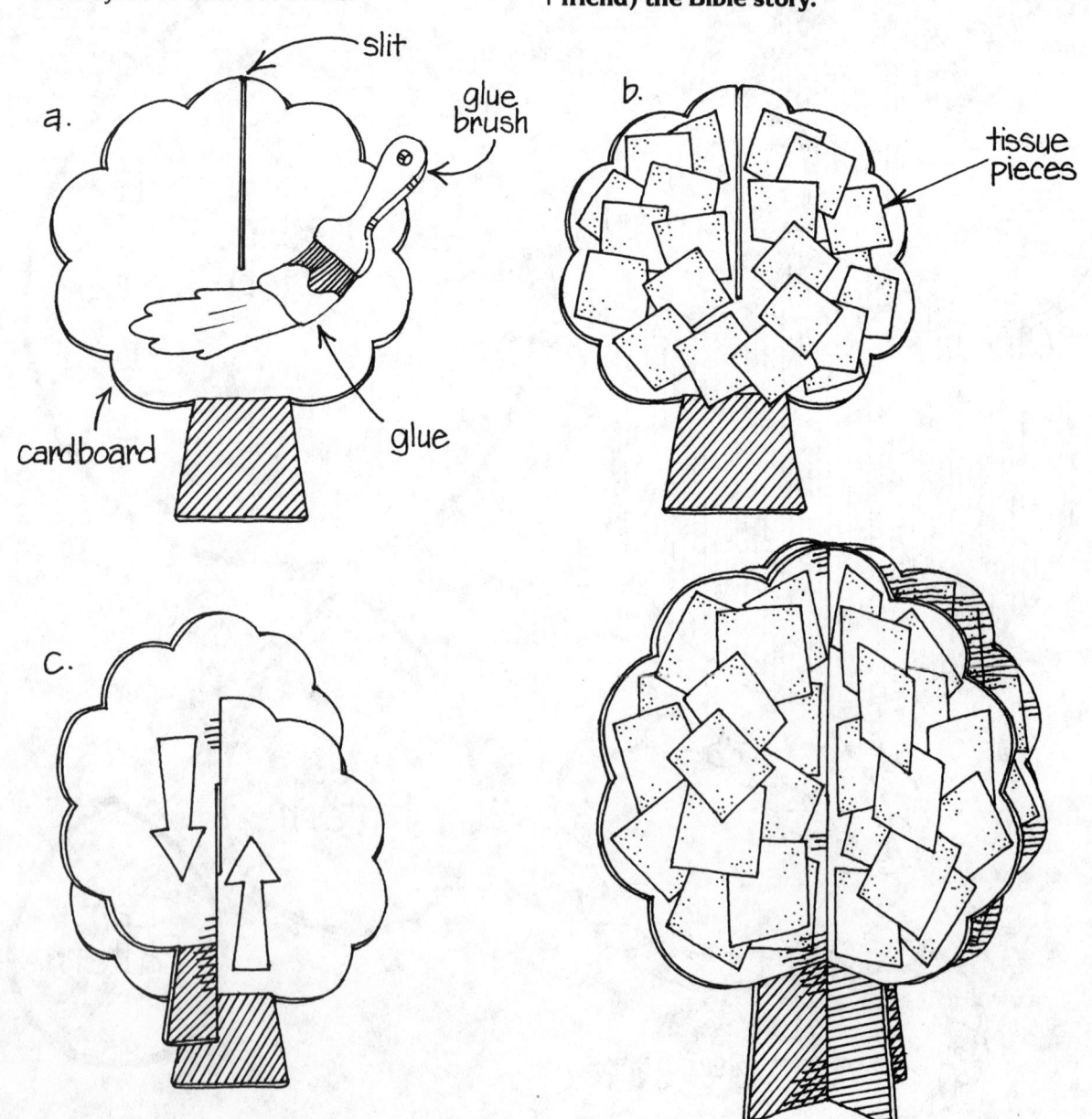

Stand-up Tree Pattern

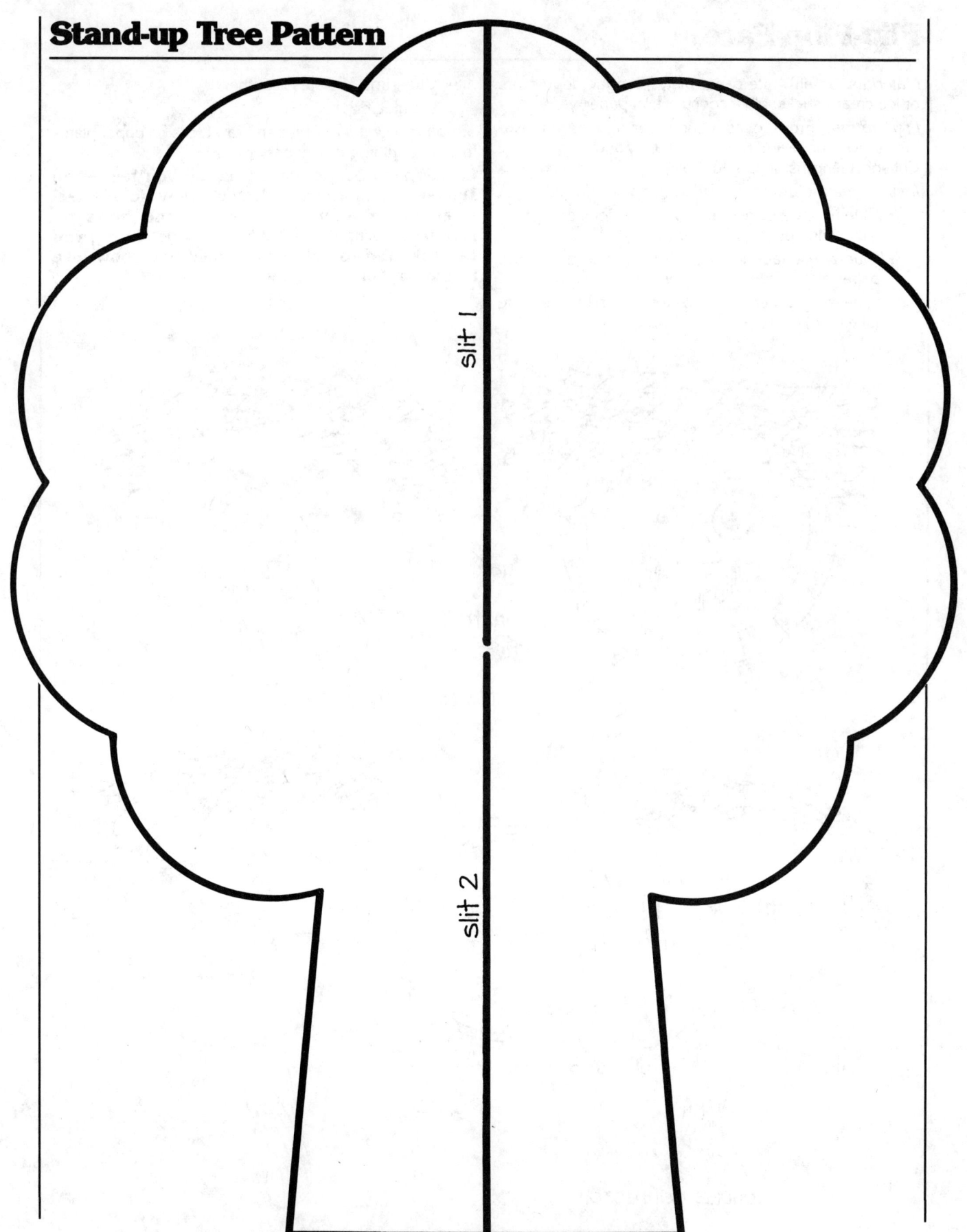

Flip-Flop Face

Materials: Small white paper plates, tongue depressors or ice cream sticks, glue, construction paper, yarn.

Preparation: From construction paper, cut out eyebrows, eyes, nose and mouth for happy and angry faces. Cut short lengths of yarn for hair.

Instruct each child in the following procedures:
- Glue happy face features to back side of one paper plate. Glue on yarn for hair (sketch a).
- Glue angry face features to back side of second paper plate. Glue on yarn for hair (sketch b).
- Glue tongue depressor to front edge of one plate (sketch c).
- Glue rims of plates together.
- Let glue dry.

Simplification Idea: Children draw faces on paper plates instead of gluing on shapes.

Conversation Suggestions: **How do you feel when someone gets angry with you? How do you feel when you make a mistake and someone shows you love instead of anger? When you get angry, you can ask God to help you forgive and show love instead of hurting others.**

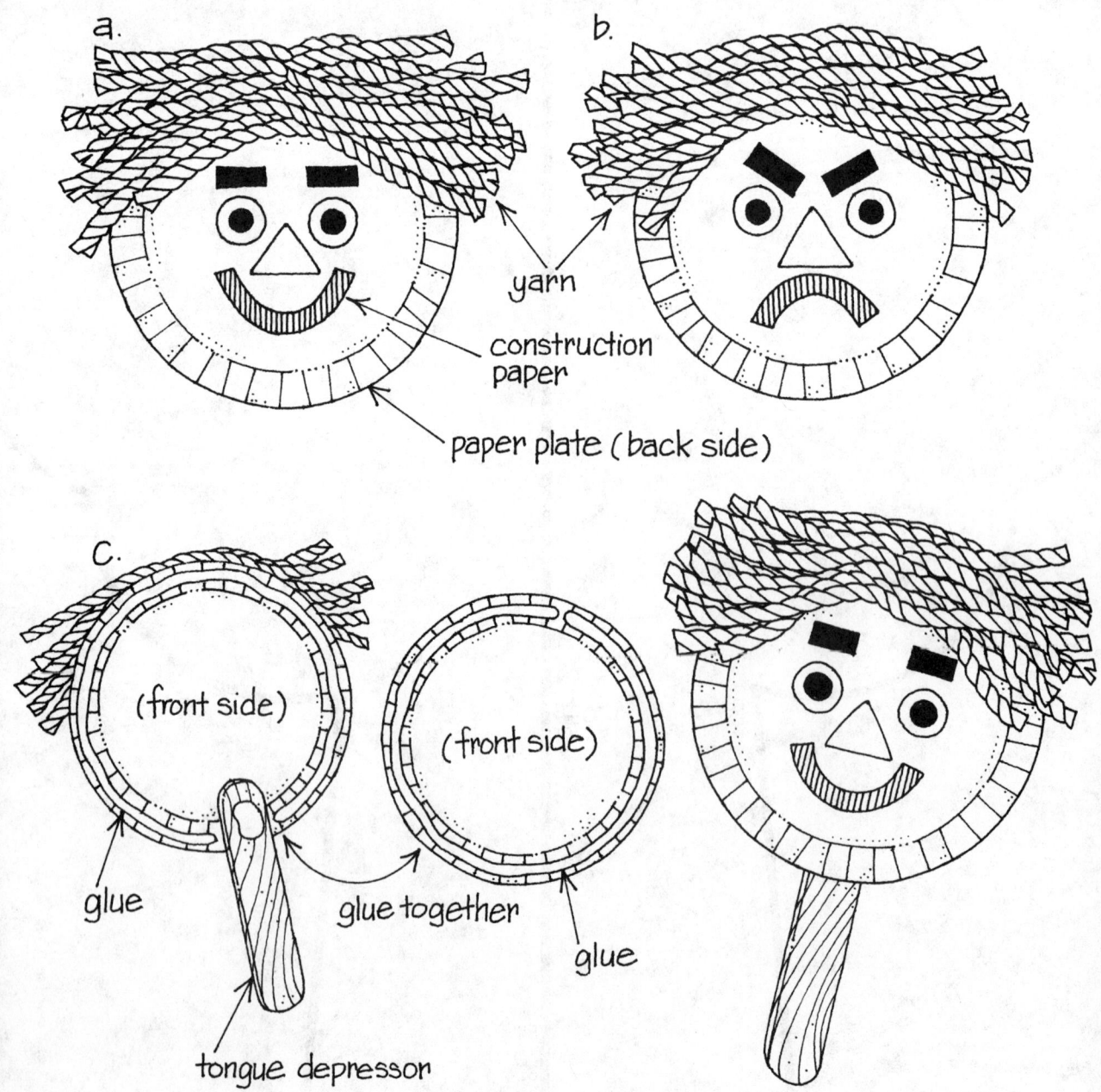

Stitch Cards

Materials: House Pattern, brightly-colored poster board, yarn, hole punch, scissors, pencil, tape, crayons. Optional—discarded magazines or catalogs, paste or glue sticks.

Preparation: Trace House Pattern onto poster board and cut out. (See "How to Make Patterns," p. 9.) Then trace poster board pattern onto poster board and cut out—one for each child. Punch holes in cards as indicated on pattern. Cut yarn into 2-foot (60-cm) lengths. Wrap tape around one end of yarn to form a "needle." Tie knot in other end of yarn (sketch a).

Instruct each child in the following procedures:

- Use crayon to draw a door and windows on house.
- Insert tape-wrapped "needle" through hole from bottom side of house. Then insert "needle" down into next hole.
- Continue sewing up and down until all holes have been used (sketch b).
- With teacher's help, tie a knot at end of yarn to secure.

Enrichment Idea: Allow children to cut out figures and faces from magazines to glue in doors and windows of houses.

Conversation Suggestions: **Who lives with you at your house? How can you show God's love to someone at home?**

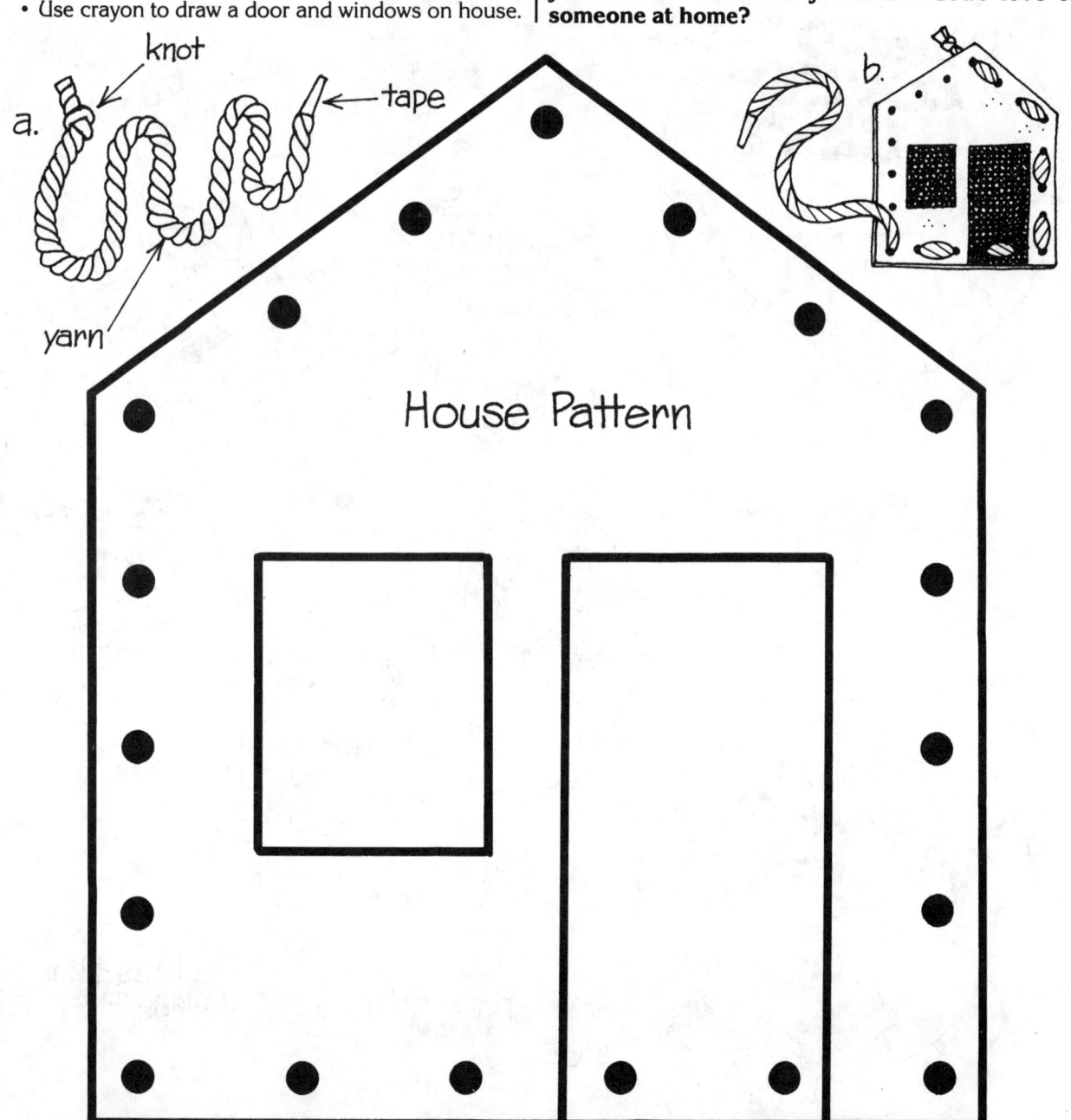

Wonder Window

Materials: Paper plates, construction paper, brad fasteners, discarded magazines, glue, ruler, felt pen or crayon.

Preparation: Cut 8-inch (20-cm) circles from construction paper—one for each child. Cut windows in paper plates (sketch a). Letter "God loves (child's name)" on plates.

Instruct each child in the following procedures:
- Find magazine pictures that illustrate ways God shows love to us (food, homes, family, nature, etc.) and cut them out.
- Glue the pictures to the construction paper circle (sketch b).
- With teacher's help, attach paper plate to circle by pushing brad through both.
- Turn wheel to see through the window different ways God shows His love to us.

Conversation Suggestions: **How does your mommy (daddy) show that she (he) loves you? How does God show that He loves you? How can you show love to others?**

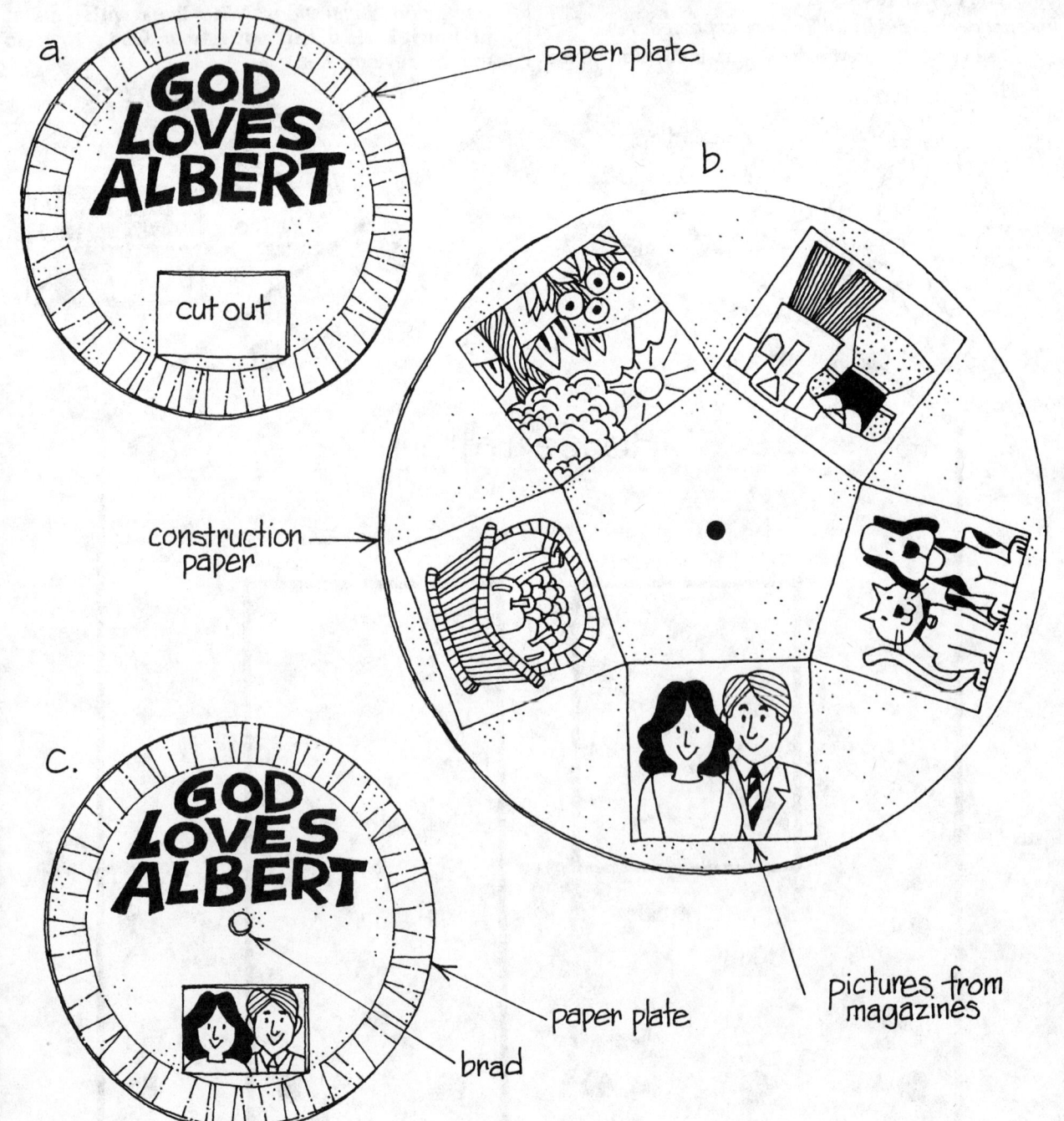

SECTION 2/GRADES 1-2

Crafts for Younger Elementary

Children in the first few years of school are delights to work with in completing craft projects. They have a handle on most of the basic skills needed, they are eager to do things and their taste in art has usually not yet surpassed their ability to produce. In other words, they generally like the things they make.

Since reading ability is not a factor in most craft projects, crafts can be a great leveler among a group. Some children excel here who may or may not be top achievers in other areas.

Many of the projects in this session also appeal to preschoolers, and as long as an adult works closely with them, they can succeed. Older children will enjoy some of these also, enjoying the fairly simple procedures required.

Sand Painting

Materials: Heavy cardboard, squeeze bottles of glue with dispenser tips, sand in a variety of colors (available in craft supply stores), large open containers for sand, spoons, drawing paper, pencils, newspapers, spray shellac or fixative, gummed picture hangers. For each student—coarse black emery paper (available at building supply stores). Optional—(materials for making your own colored sand) water, fine sand, powdered fabric dyes, containers in which to dye sand, paper towels, newspapers.

Preparation: Pour colored sand into large open containers (so children have easy access to sand).

Optional—(to dye sand) fill containers one-half to two-thirds full of sand—one container for each color of powdered fabric dye. Add water to cover sand completely. Add a spoonful of powdered fabric dye. Stir and let sit for fifteen minutes. Then carefully pour out as much water as possible without losing the sand. Spoon sand onto newspaper pads covered with paper toweling and spread to dry for 12-24 hours.

For each student, cut a cardboard piece slightly larger than a sheet of emery paper. Glue the sheet of emery paper, black side up, to cardboard. Cover work area with newspapers.

Instruct each child in the following procedures:

- On paper, draw a simple design such as an island with a palm tree.
- Copy one part of your design onto emery paper, using glue to draw lines (sketch a). Fill in outline with glue if desired.
- Spoon one color of sand over glue (sketch b). Work with only one color of sand at a time.
- Turn picture on edge and tap lightly over container to remove excess sand (sketch c).
- Repeat process for each color of sand used.
- For more texture, let dry and repeat glueing and sanding to build up the area.
- When picture is dry, spray with fixative or shellac.
- Add gummed picture hanger to back.

Conversation Suggestions: **Have you ever visited an island? God created beautiful places like islands for people to enjoy because He loves us. What is another way God has shown His love for us?**

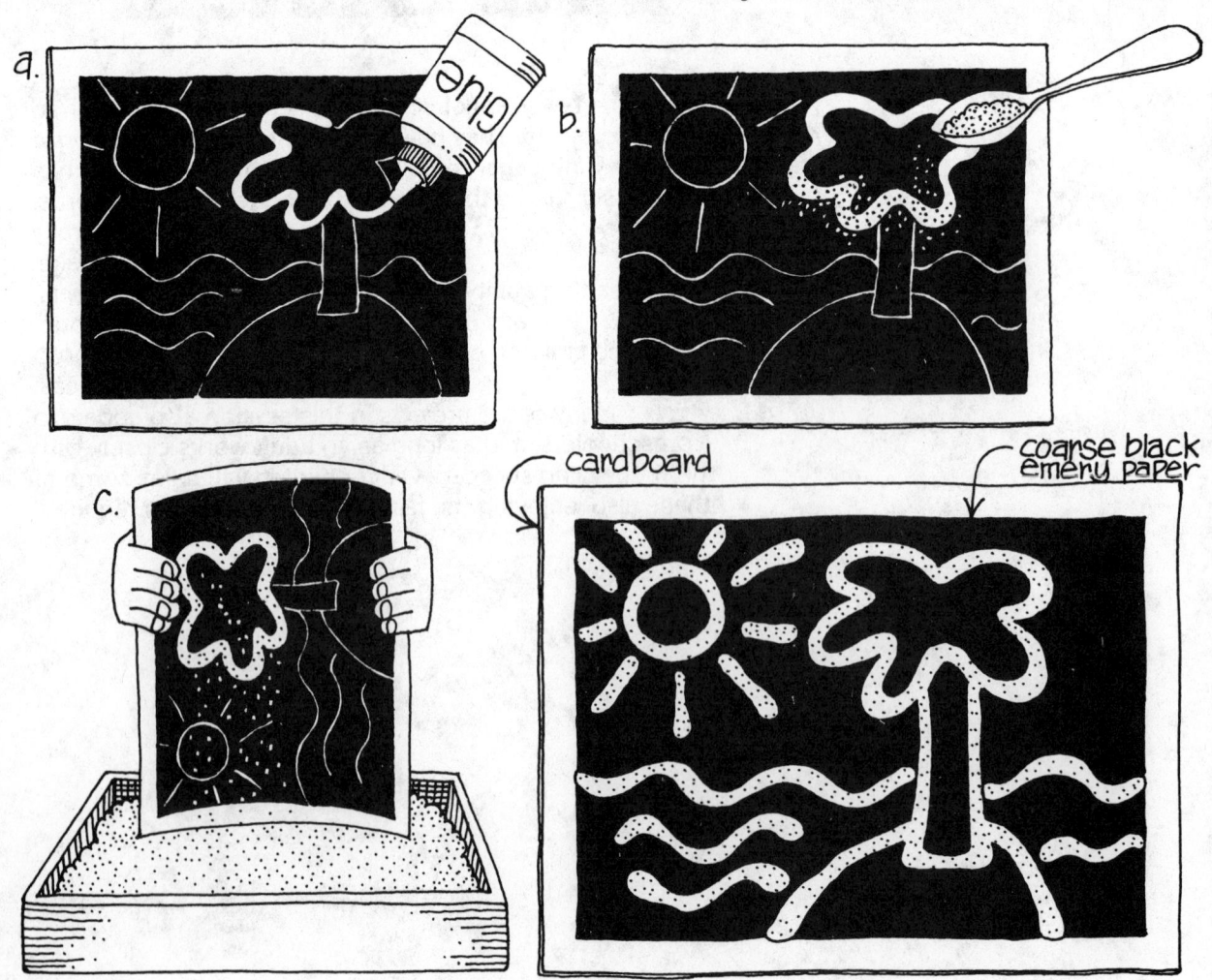

24

Good Samaritan Doll

Materials: Felt pens, heavy yarn, tacky glue, fabric, scissors, large wiggle eyes. For each child—plastic detergent bottle, 3-inch (7.5-cm) Styrofoam ball (available at craft store). Optional—sand.

Preparation: Wash and dry bottles. (Optional—fill bottles with sand for stability.) Cut yarn into 4-inch (10-cm) lengths for man's hair and 2-inch (5-cm) lengths for beard. Cut yarn into 14-inch (35-cm) lengths for belt—one for each child. Cut fabric into 5 × 18-inch (12.5 × 45-cm) rectangles—one for each child. Cut opening in fabric (sketch a).

Instruct each child in the following procedures:
- Slip fabric over bottle (sketch b).
- Tie yarn around waist for belt (sketch c).
- Place line of glue around rim of bottle neck. Push Styrofoam ball onto bottle neck.
- Use felt pen to draw nose and mouth on ball.
- Glue on wiggle eyes.
- Glue yarn to head for hair and beard.

Conversation Suggestions: **Which person in our Bible story could this doll be? What did you learn about that person?**

Butterfly

Materials: Light-colored construction paper, 10-inch (25-cm) pieces of chenille wire, 6-inch (15-cm) squares of brightly-colored tissue paper, felt pens or crayons, pencils, glue or tape.

Instruct each child in the following procedures:
- With teacher's help, twist chenille wire to form bottom half of butterfly body (sketch a).
- Fold tissue paper accordion style.
- Place the folded tissue on the twisted chenille wire (sketch b).
- Twist wire two or three more times to form upper half of butterfly body (sketch c).
- Wrap chenille wire around the pencil to make the antennas.
- Glue or tape butterfly to construction paper.
- Use crayons or felt pens to draw flowers on bottom of page.

Conversation Suggestions: **Danny, I saw you helping Greg make his butterfly. Lisa, you were helping Tricia. When we help others we are showing God's love. Who showed God's love in our Bible story? How can you show God's love by helping at home?**

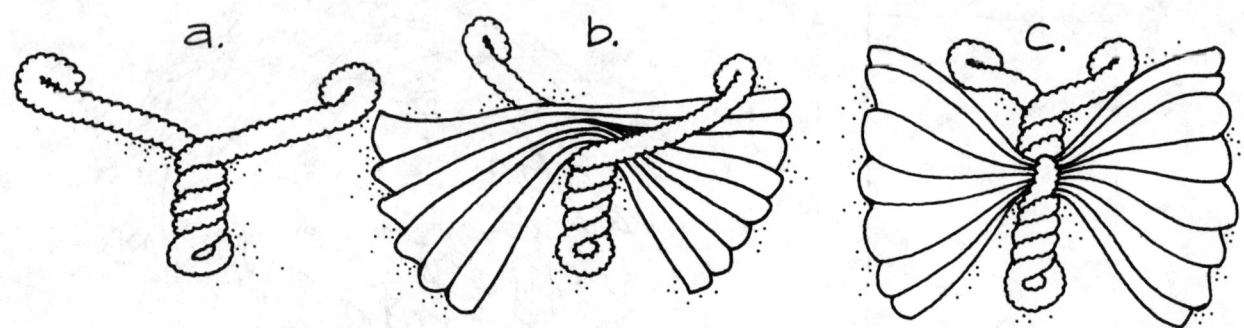

26

Kindness Kritter Pencil

Materials: Can Cover Pattern, construction paper, photocopy machine, felt pens, ruler, white glue, fake fur, yarn, small wiggle eyes, scissors. For each child—one small juice can, one new pencil.

Preparation: Wash and dry juice cans. Cut 2×3-inch (5×7.5-cm) rectangles from fake fur—one for each child. Photocopy Can Cover Pattern onto construction paper—one for each child. Cut yarn into 6-inch (15-cm) lengths.

Instruct each child in the following procedures:
- Place a line of glue down each inside end of fur piece (sketch a).
- Wrap fur around eraser end of pencil and secure with yarn (sketch b).
- Glue wiggle eyes on fur.
- Color letters on Can Cover Pattern. Cut out can cover.
- Glue can cover to can.
- Place Kindness Kritter Pencil in pencil holder.

Conversation Suggestions: **Who is someone who has been kind to you? How did you feel? First Corinthians 13:4a says, "Love is patient, love is kind." What would be a kind thing you could do with your Kindness Kritter?** (Let someone use it, write a note to someone.)

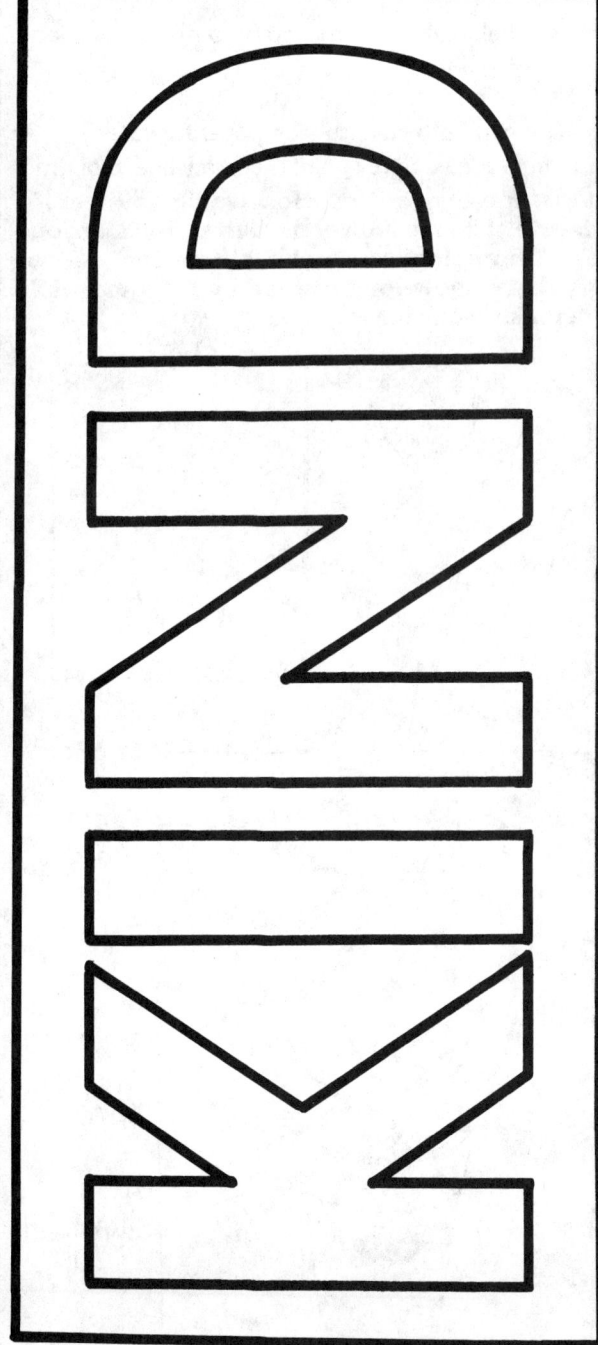

Can Cover Pattern

Thumbprint Creature

Materials: Stamp pads (one for each table), black fine-tip felt pens, hole punch, 1/4-inch (6.25-mm) ribbon, disposable towelettes. For each child—a small, white, non-waxed paper plate.

Preparation: Cut ribbon into 16-inch (40-cm) lengths—one for each child.

Instruct each child in the following procedures:

- Press thumb on ink pad and then press in center of paper plate. Add additional thumbprints to make a creature or person. Use towelette to clean thumb.
- Use felt pen to draw eyes, nose, feet, etc.
- Punch two holes at top of paper plate.
- Thread ribbon through holes and tie.

Conversation Suggestions: **What is a way to show love while making your Thumbprint Creatures?** (Share supplies, compliment someone.) **You can share God's love anytime, anywhere!**

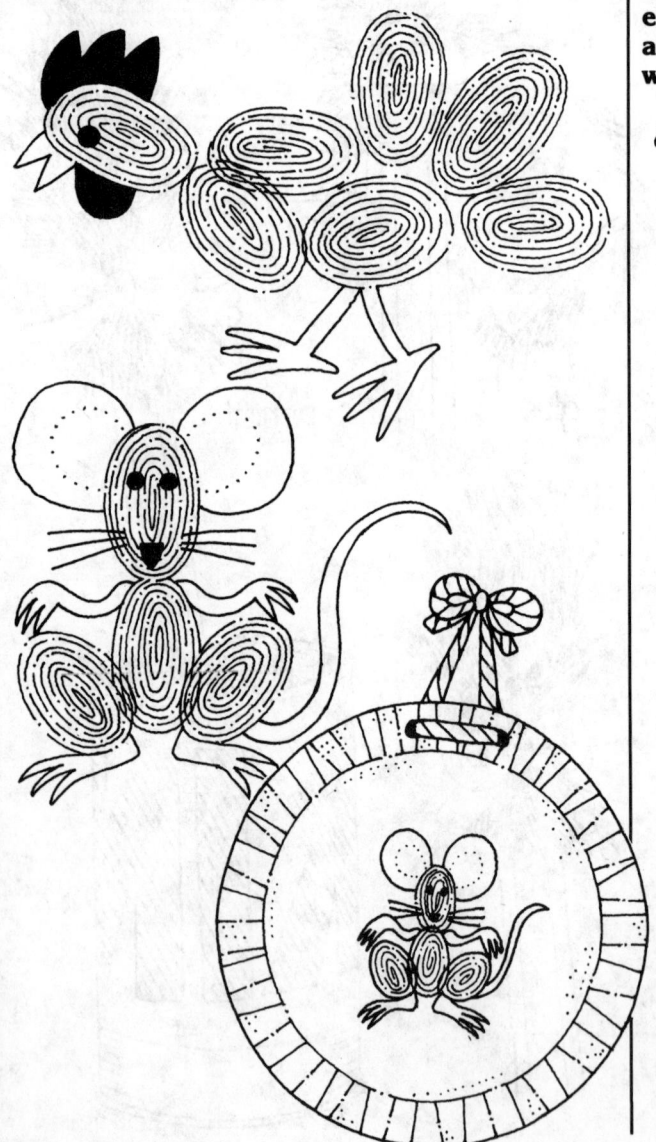

Daisy Flower

Materials: Small Styrofoam cups, felt pens, elbow macaroni, shell macaroni, glue, construction paper, scissors, pencil, green chenille wire for stems. Optional—spray paint.

Preparation: Cut paper cup in half from top to bottom (sketch a). Draw outline of cup on each piece of construction paper (sketch b).

Instruct each child in the following procedures:

- Glue chenille wire onto paper with end extending into "vase."
- Use shell and elbow macaroni to make flower and leaves on stem.
- Use felt pens to decorate cup.
- Glue cup onto construction paper for vase.

Enrichment Ideas: Spray paint macaroni ahead of time.

Conversation Suggestions: **How would you feel if I said, "Ha, ha. My flower is better than anyone else's?"** Bragging can make others feel sad or angry. Let's show love instead of bragging while we're making our flowers.

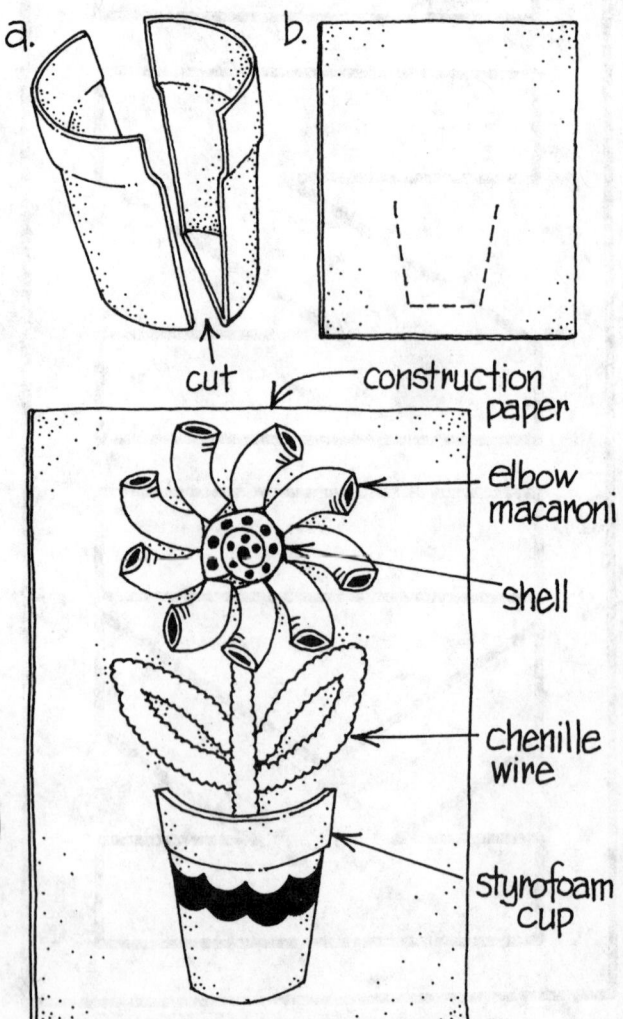

Love Stencil Poster

Materials: Stencil Patterns, scissors, old toothbrushes, several small pieces of screen, several colors of dry tempera paint, shallow containers, sponges, paper towels, shallow cardboard boxes, newspapers, painting smocks or old shirts, masking tape, construction paper.

Preparation: Photocopy Stencil Patterns onto construction paper—one pattern for every two or three children. Cut out stencils. Mix dry tempera paint with small amount of water in shallow containers. (Paint should be thick so it will not run under stencil.) Cover work area with newspapers.

Instruct each child in the following procedures:
- Put on painting smock or old shirt.
- Place construction paper in bottom of box.
- Tape stencil frame onto paper with masking tape.
- Dip toothbrush in paint and brush on screen to spatter paint on paper (see sketch).
- Carefully remove stencil to prevent smearing.
- Allow paint to dry.

Enrichment Idea: Child may use different stencils in various positions on the paper, using various colors of paint.

Conversation Suggestions: **When is it hardest for you to show love? Hang your poster in a place where it will remind you to show God's love** (at home, school, etc.).

Love Stencil Poster Patterns

Love Stencil Poster Patterns

Hymnbook

Materials: Music Note Pattern, lightweight cardboard, white 8½ × 11-inch (21.25 × 27.5-cm) unlined paper, various colors of construction paper, construction paper (cut to fit the white paper), soft-lead pencil, scissors, stapler and staples, crayons or felt pens, glue, chalkboard and chalk (or newsprint and felt marker).

Preparation: Trace Music Note Pattern onto cardboard. (See "How to Make Patterns," p. 9.) Cut out. Using soft-lead pencil, trace music note onto construction paper—two or more for each child. Letter words to one or two short songs about God's love on chalkboard or newsprint.

Instruct each child in the following procedures:
- Cut out music notes.
- Fold white paper and construction paper in half putting short sides together.
- Place white paper inside construction paper to form book.
- With teacher's help, staple along fold line of book.
- On front cover, letter "Hymns" or "Psalms."
- Glue one music note on front cover.
- Open book and glue one or more music notes inside.
- Letter words of songs on white pages.
- Use crayons or felt pens to draw illustrations as desired.

Enrichment Idea: Children may compose their own song lyrics as ability or desire indicates.

Conversation Suggestions: **When I think of how much God loves me, it makes me very happy. And when I'm happy, I like to sing. We can use our songbooks when we're happy and want to sing.**

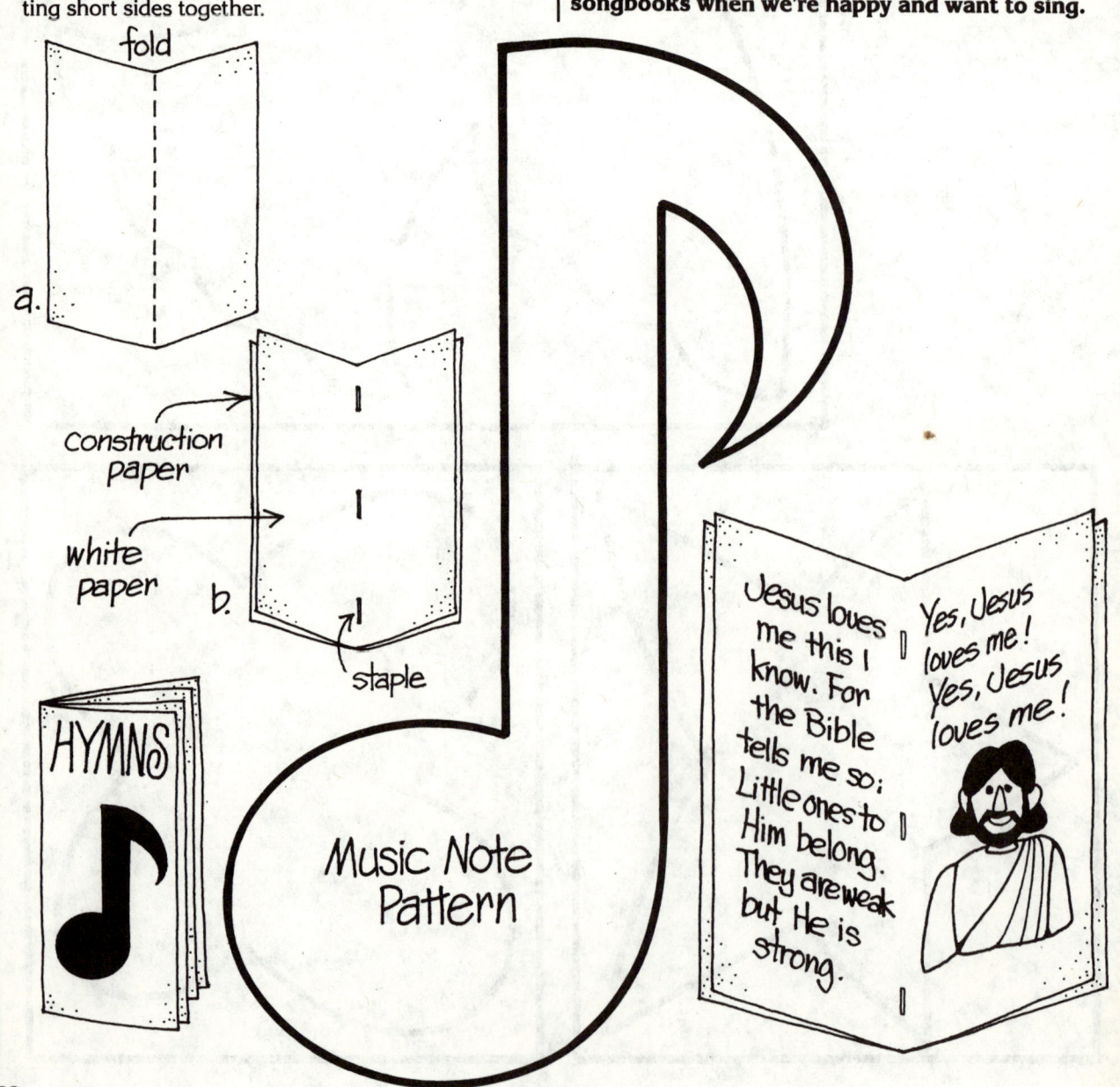

32

Hanging Holder

Materials: Various colors of stamp pads, disposable towelettes, hole punch, felt pens, scissors, tape, paper plates, brightly-colored yarn.

Preparation: Cut enough paper plates in half so each child has one half. Lay half plates on top of whole plates and punch holes (sketch b)—one set for each child. Cut yarn into 48-inch (120-cm) lengths—one for each child. Wrap one end of each length of yarn with tape to form "needle." Knot each length of yarn 12-inches (30-cm) from end.

Instruct each child in the following procedures:

- Thread yarn up through first hole, then up through second hole. (The loose end of the yarn will be used as a hanger.) Continue until the plates are sewn together (sketch c).
- Tie yarn together at ends (sketch d).
- Decorate holder with felt pens and ink thumbprints.
- Letter a Bible verse on the holder.

Conversation Suggestions: **Who can say the Bible verse we learned today? Where can you hang your Hanging Holder to remind you of this verse?**

Angel Bookmark

Materials: Angel Bookmark Pattern, lightweight poster board, scissors, felt pens, various colors of grosgrain ribbon, ruler, staples, stapler, glue.

Preparation: Trace Angel Bookmark Pattern onto poster board and cut out—one for each child. Cut ribbon for streamers into 6-inch (15-cm) lengths—four for each child. Cut ribbon for waistbands into 3-inch (7.5-cm) lengths—one for each child.

Instruct each child in the following procedures:
- Use felt pens to draw the angel's facial features and hair.
- Staple the ribbon streamers to the waist of the angel (sketch a).
- Glue ribbon waistband over staples to hide raw edges (sketch b).
- Glue ends of waistband to back of bookmark (sketch c).
- To use as a bookmark, place arms of angel across page you want to mark (sketch d).

Conversation Suggestions: **What did the angel in our Bible story do? Can you find the story in your Bible and mark it with your Angel Bookmark?**

Angel Bookmark Pattern

SECTION 3/GRADES 3-6

Crafts for Older Elementary

Trying to plan craft projects for older children has driven many teachers prematurely grey. The challenge is that while these children have well-developed skills to complete projects, they also have well-developed preferences about what they want to do. Thus a project that may challenge their abilities may be scorned because it somehow is not appealing to these young sophisticates. Then the next project will seem juvenile to the adult, but will click with the kids!

There's no justice! And a sense of humor surely helps. One helpful device is to filter a craft idea through a panel of experts—two or three sixth graders. If they like it, chances are the rest of the group will, also. Then, the better you get to know your particular students, the better your batting average will be.

And most of the time, most of the group will thoroughly enjoy the projects in this section. They have been tested under fire and came out with colors flying and only a few tatters.

Island in the Son Plaque

(Two-Day Project)

Materials: Plaster of paris (½ lb. for each child), coffee cans, paint stirring sticks, sand, yellow poster board, waxed paper, poster or acrylic paints, paintbrushes, gummed picture hangers, scissors, felt pens, water, measuring cup.

Instruct each student in the following procedures:

- Ask children what an island looks like. Show pictures of islands to provide additional ideas.
- Assign each child a partner. (Children work together to prepare plaster.) Give each pair of children a stirring stick, two large pieces of waxed paper and a coffee can filled half way with dry plaster of paris.
- Assist children in mixing water with plaster according to package directions. (Supervise closely!) Plaster should look like thin cream.
- Quickly stir enough sand into the plaster to make the mixture look like thick whipped cream.
- Pour the plaster mixture onto waxed paper, forming an island shape (sketch a). Use fingers to form details. Work quickly, before plaster sets. Sprinkle sand on "land" portion of wet plaster. Allow to dry overnight.
- The following day, add detail and color to island with paints and remove from waxed paper.
- Cut a rising sun shape from yellow poster board. Letter on it, "God sent His Son, Jesus," and glue to back of plaster island (sketch b).
- Affix gummed picture hanger to back of island with glue (hanger will not stick by itself).

Conversation Suggestions: **The Bible tells us that God loves us even more than our friends and families love us. What are some things God has done to show us how much He loves us?** (Children respond.) **You can hang your *Island in the Son* on a wall to remind you of the biggest and best thing God did to show His love.**

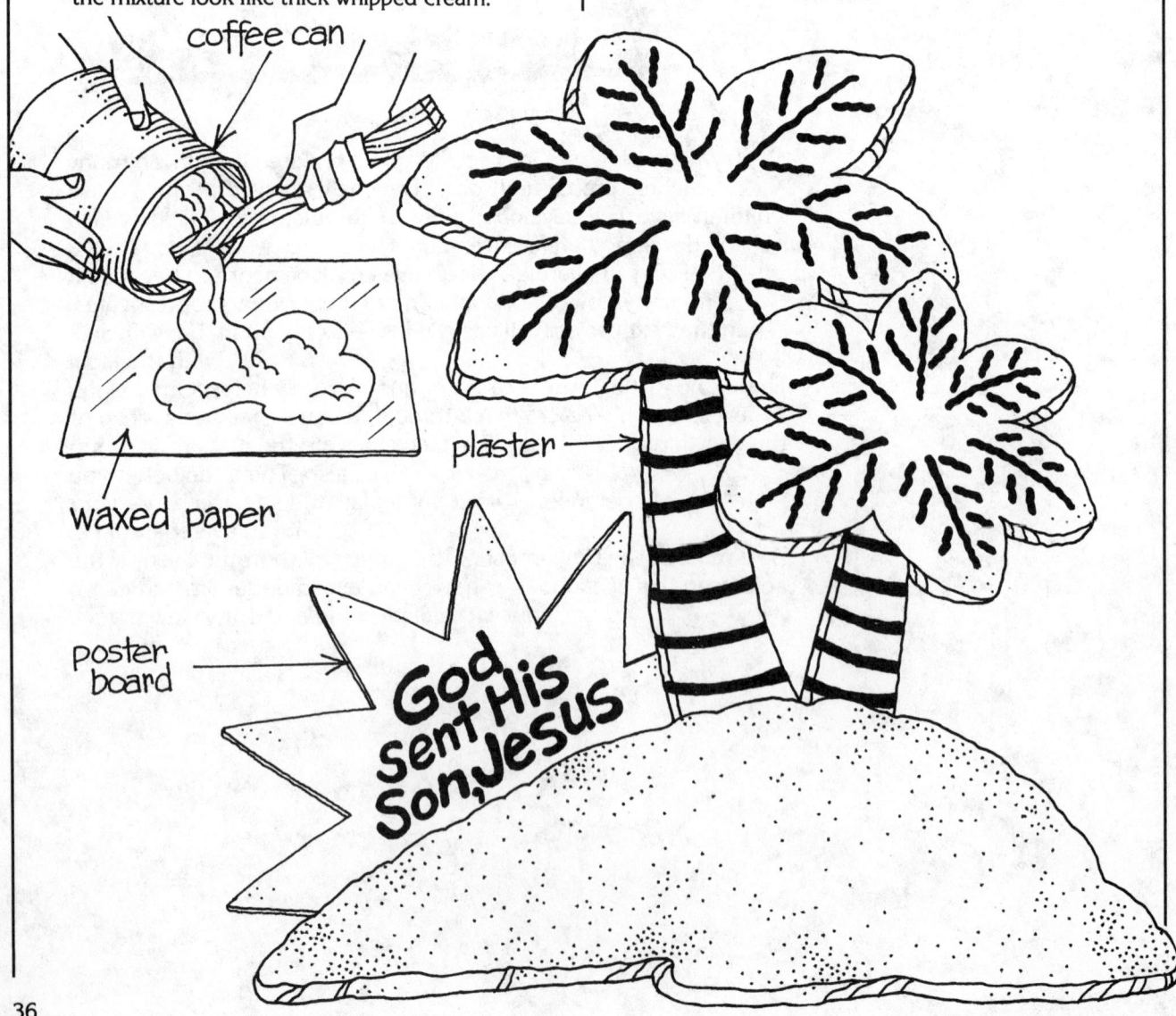

Goofy Glasses

Materials: Plastic carriers from soft-drink six-packs, scissors, colored cloth or paper, fake fur, glue, tape, chenille wires (two for each student).

Preparation: Cut apart plastic carriers (sketch a). Make a sample pair of glasses, following directions below.

Instruct each student in the following procedures:
- Attach a chenille wire to each side of plastic rim for ear pieces.
- Cut noses, mustaches, eyebrows or decorative rims from paper, fake fur or cloth.
- Use glue and/or tape to attach decorations to plastic rims.

Conversation Suggestions: **Why do you think it's important for people in God's family to show love through actions? What are some ways you might show love as we are working on our Goofy Glasses?**

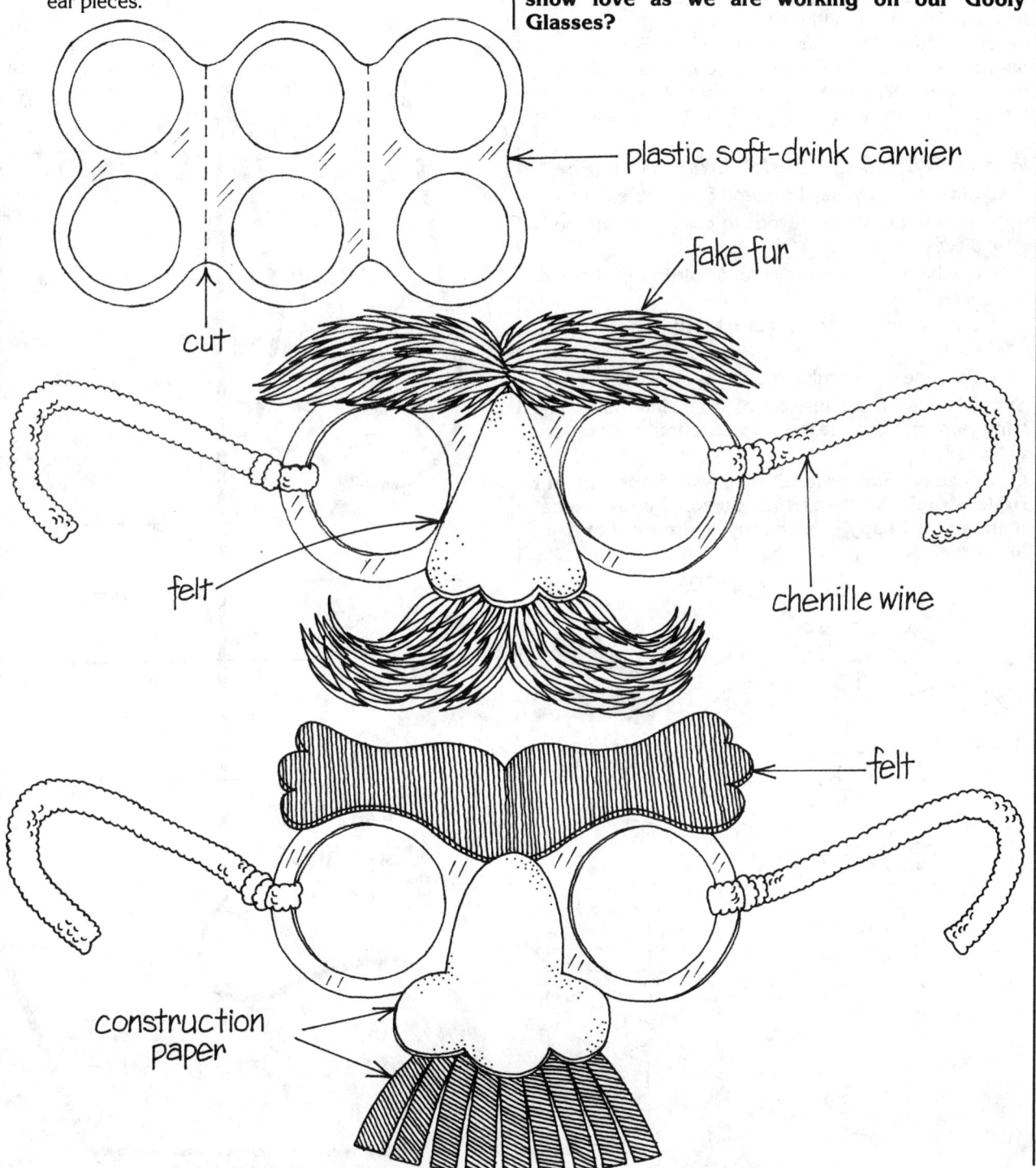

Happy Man Mobile

Materials: Happy Man Face and Body Patterns, poster board, 8 × 10-inch (20 × 25-cm) and 12 × 18-inch (30 × 45-cm) sheets of heavy white paper, felt pens, crayons, yarn, scissors, pencils, ruler, masking tape, photocopy machine.

Preparation: Photocopy Happy Man Face Patterns onto smaller sheets of white paper—one for each child. Enlarge Happy Man Body Pattern, trace onto poster board and cut out. Fold 12 × 18-inch (30 × 45-cm) white paper in half vertically. Trace Happy Man Body Pattern onto each folded sheet, indicating cut lines by drawing dotted lines. Make one for each child. Make a sample Happy Man Mobile to show students how to assemble pieces.

Instruct each student in the following procedures:
- Cut out Happy Man Face and Body pieces.
- Use felt pens and crayons to color face and body pieces.
- Use hole punch to punch one hole in top center of each piece.
- Cut yarn into 4-inch (10-cm) lengths and tie one to each hole.
- Use tape to assemble mobile as shown in sketch.

Simplification Idea: Instead of punching holes and tying yarn, children use tape to fasten both ends of yarn to face pieces.

Conversation Suggestions: **Who was happy in our Bible story? Why was this person happy? What makes you happy? I'm happy to know that God loves me.**

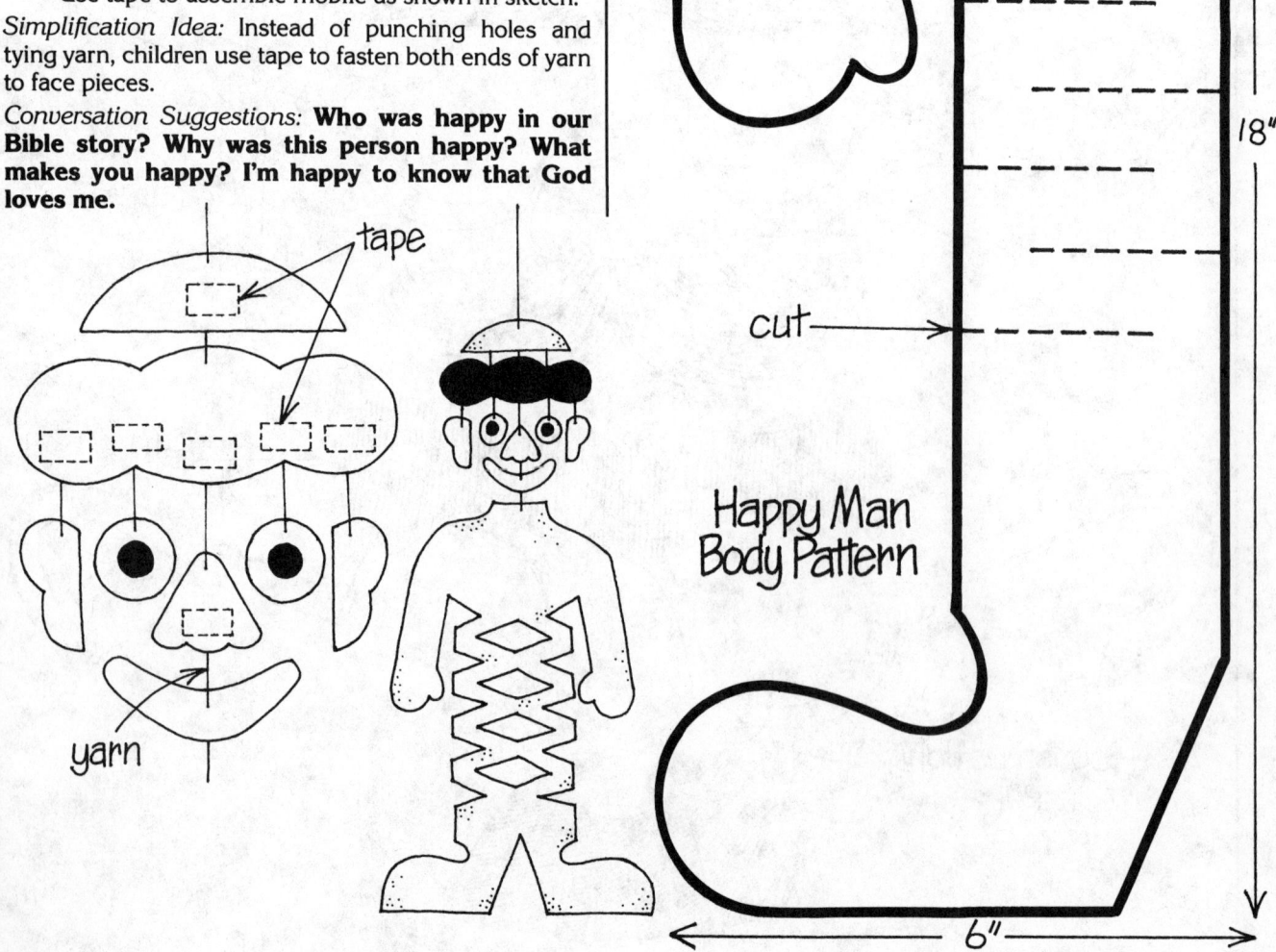

38

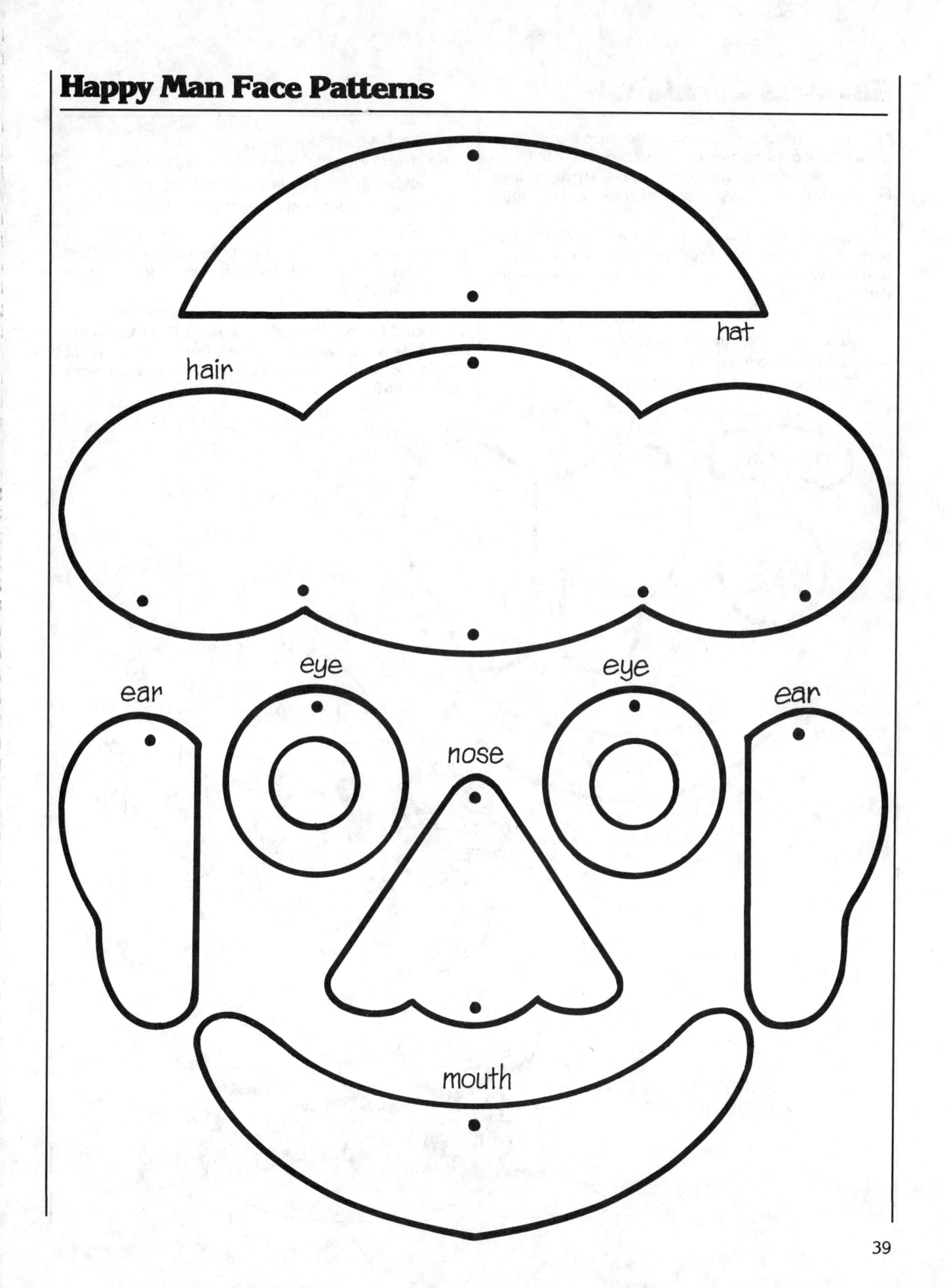

Happy Man Face Patterns

hat

hair

eye eye

ear nose ear

mouth

39

Kindness Cookie Tub

Materials: Eye, Eyebrow, Ear and Mouth Patterns, lightweight cardboard, pom-poms, various colors of felt, fake fur, glue, scissors, permanant felt pens, small cookies. For each child—32 oz. plastic margarine tub, two wiggle eyes.

Preparation: Trace Eye, Eyebrow, Ear and Mouth Patterns onto cardboard and cut out. Make one of each pattern for every two to three students. (See "How to Make Patterns," p. 9.)

Instruct each student in the following procedures:
- Trace around margarine lid onto felt and cut out.
- Glue circle to top of lid.
- Trace patterns onto felt and cut out.
- Glue felt pieces to "face."
- Glue on wiggle eyes and pom-pom nose.
- Cut fake fur for hair and glue to head.
- Decorate sides of plastic tub with felt pens.
- Fill tub with cookies.

Simplification Idea: Photocopy patterns onto construction paper. Children cut facial features out of paper, instead of using felt.

Conversation Suggestions: **Name a person who has been kind to you. How did you feel? First Corinthians 13:4a says,** *Love is patient, love is kind.* **What would be a kind thing you could do with your cookie tub?**

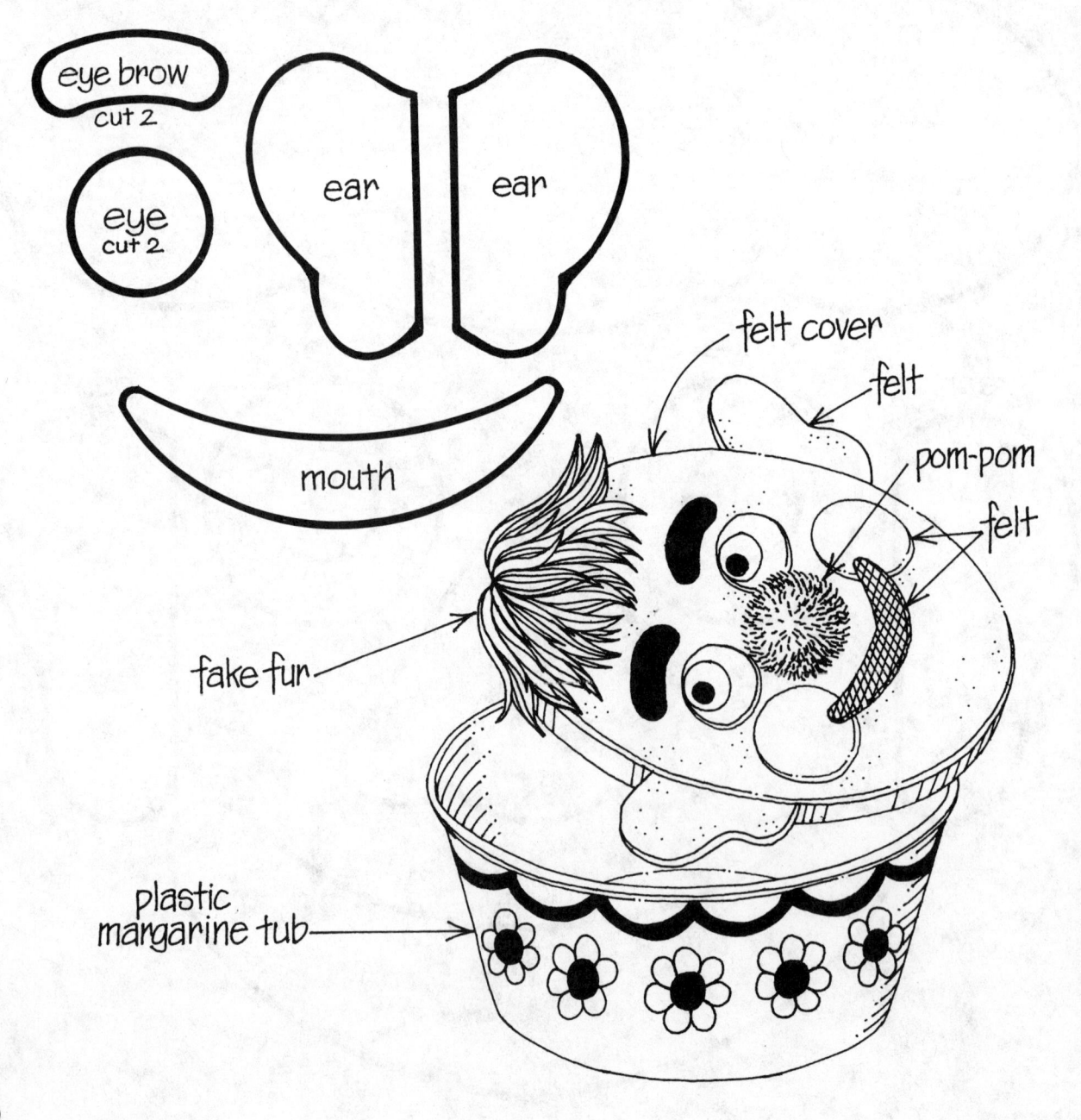

Wooden Key Holder

Materials: Catalogs, magazines or old calendars with pictures, 1-inch (2.5-cm) plywood, screw-in hooks, sandpaper, wood stain, clear acrylic spray, electric drill, jigsaw, glue, scissors, hammer, nail, cloth scraps.

Preparation: Use jigsaw to cut plywood in shape shown in sketch—one for each child. Drill hole in top for hanging. Use hammer and nail to make four holes deep enough for hooks (sketch a). Cut ribbon into 12-inch (30-cm) lengths—one for each child.

Instruct each student in the following procedures:
- Use sandpaper to sand wood shape.
- Dip cloth in stain and rub on front and sides of wood. Let dry.
- Cut picture from magazine and glue to wood shape (sketch b). Allow glue to dry.
- Spray the wood and the picture with acrylic spray (sketch c).
- Screw hooks into holes.
- Thread ribbon through hole and tie (sketch d).

Conversation Suggestions: **Do any of our key holders look exactly the same? No, each one is different. God made each person different, too. Since there is something special about each one of us, we don't need to envy others. Instead, we can thank God for the special way He made each of us.**

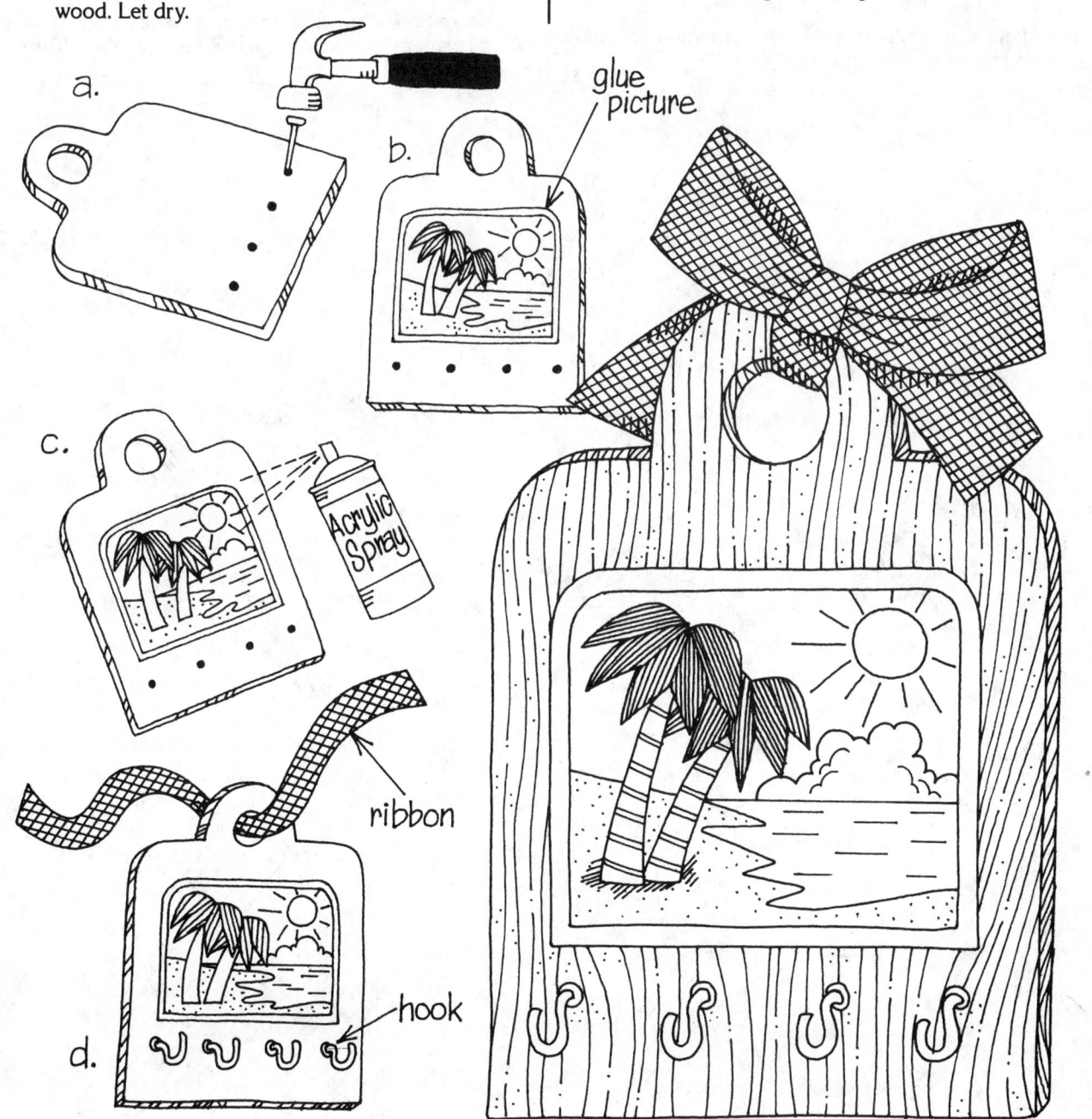

Gift Potpourri Pouch

Materials: Grater, oranges, lemons, allspice, cloves, cinnamon oil and sticks, calico fabric, ruler, pens, pinking shears, wide and narrow ribbon, small plastic cups, plastic spoons, 2-inch (5-cm) ribbon, D-rings, white glue, rubber bands.

Preparation: Cut a 4-inch (10-cm) diameter circle pattern for each student (sketch a). Cut wider ribbon into 12-inch (30-cm) lengths—one for each student. Cut narrow ribbon into 10-inch (25-cm) lengths—one for each student.

Instruct each student in the following procedures:
- Fold wider ribbon over ring and glue (sketch b). Let dry. Cut end of ribbon into inverted V shape.
- Grate a spoonful of peel from orange and lemon and place in plastic cup.
- Add to cup a spoonful of allspice and cloves and several drops of cinnamon oil. Use plastic spoon to mix ingredients together.
- Trace around circle pattern onto calico cloth and cut out circle using pinking shears.
- Place potpourri in center of fabric circle (sketch c).
- Gather ends of circle together and fasten with rubber band.
- Lay pouch on ribbon hanger and tie a knot with narrow ribbon (sketch d).
- Place cinnamon stick on top of knot, then tie bow (sketch e).

Conversation Suggestions: **Who is proud of what he or she made? I'm glad you like what you made! What is a way you can express your pride without bragging?**

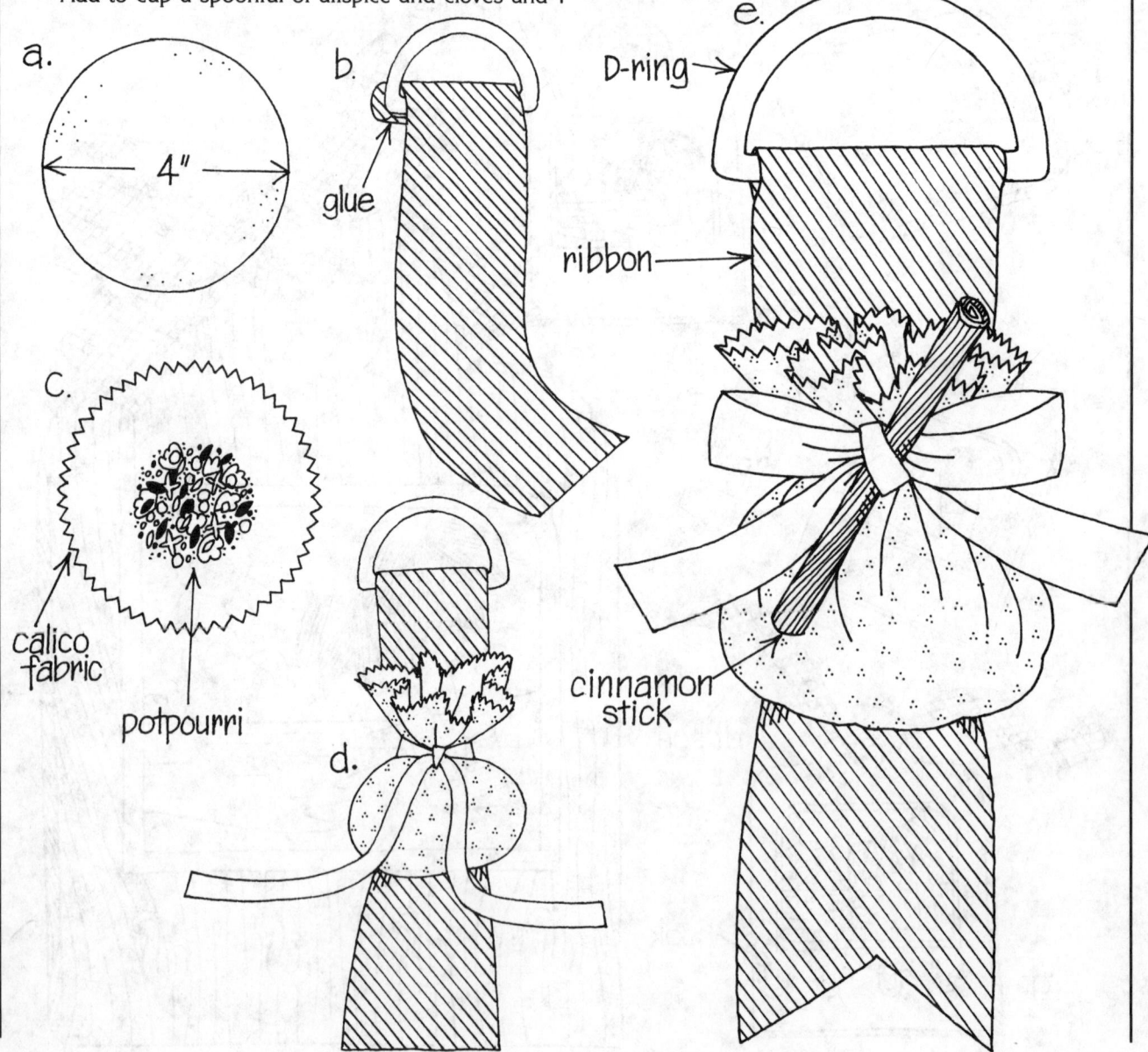

Bread Dough Napkin Rings

Materials: Heart and Dove Napkin Ring Patterns, lightweight cardboard, pencil, scissors, large bowl, small bowl, measuring cup, teaspoon, wooden spoon, flour (NOT self-rising), cornstarch, salt, glycerin, water, rolling pins, cookie sheet, clear acrylic spray, oven, dull kitchen knife, acrylic paint, paintbrushes.

Preparation: Trace Heart and Dove Patterns onto lightweight cardboard. (See "How to Make Patterns," p. 9.) Cut one pattern for every two or three students. Make dough using the following recipe: Mix 2 cups flour, 1 cup cornstarch and 1 cup salt in the larger bowl. In the smaller bowl, mix 1 tsp. glycerin and 1 cup water. Combine wet and dry ingredients. Knead for 5 minutes until smooth. Recipe makes enough for eight to twelve napkin rings.

Instruct each student in the following procedures:

- Use rolling pin to flatten dough to ¼-inch (6.25-mm) thickness (sketch a).
- Lay Heart or Dove Pattern on dough and cut out shape with knife (sketch b).
- For interesting designs, use tip of pencil to make light impressions in dough (sketch c).
- Place napkin rings on cookie sheet and bake in 275 degrees Fahrenheit (135 degrees Celcius) oven for one hour.
- Turn oven off and allow napkin rings to cool in oven for one hour to eliminate cracking.
- Use acrylic paints to decorate napkin rings. Let the rings dry.
- Spray napkin rings with clear acrylic spray.

Conversation Suggestions: **First Corinthians 13:5 says, *Love is not self-seeking.* What does it mean to be self-seeking? Sometimes it is hard to be unselfish at home. When you and your family use these napkin rings, they can remind you to be unselfish.**

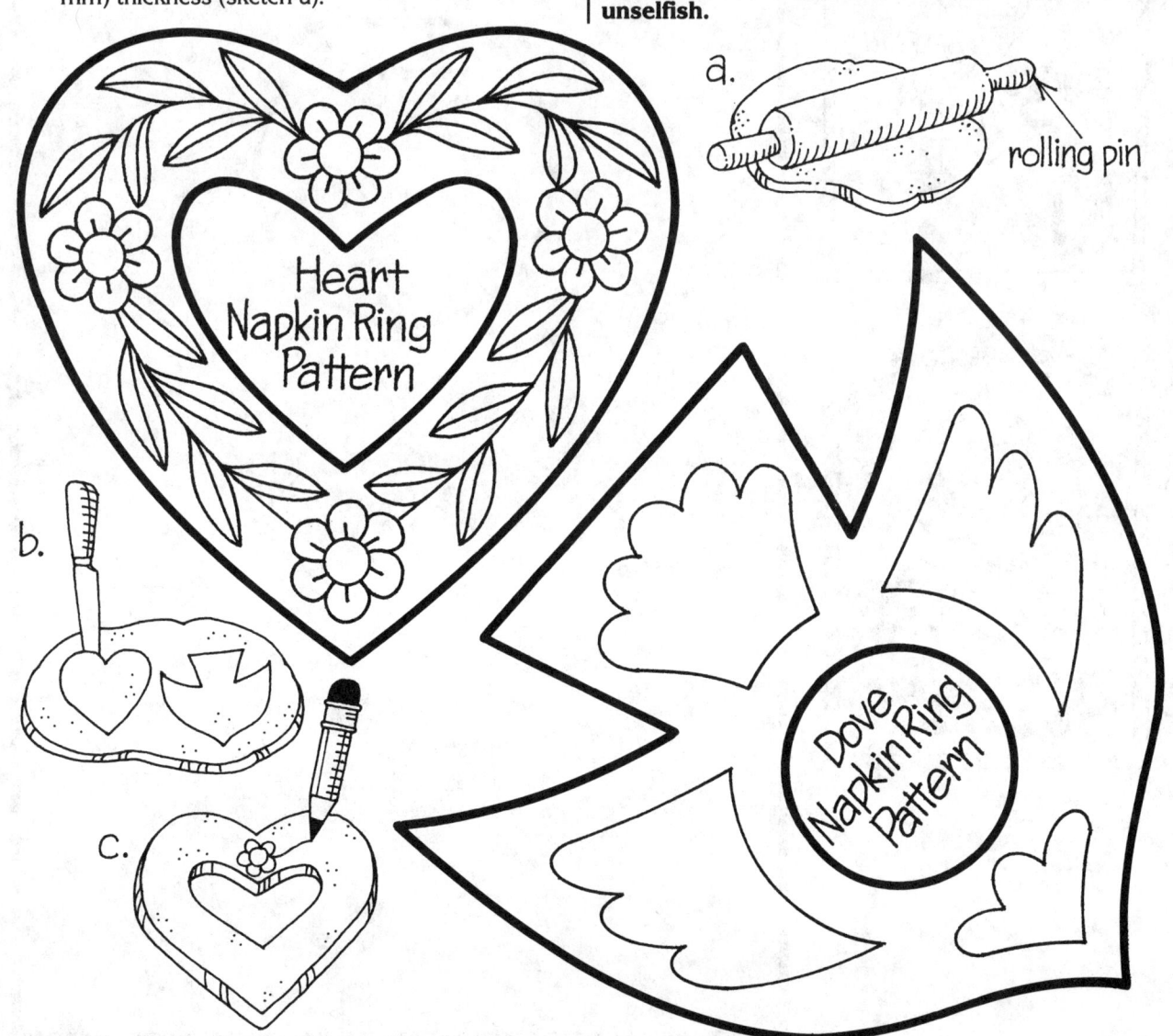

Doorknob Hanger

Materials: Doorknob Hanger Pattern, lightweight cardboard, pencil, felt pens, white tagboard, yarn, glue, scissors.

Preparation: Trace pattern onto cardboard and cut out. (See "How to Make Patterns," p. 9.) Trace pattern onto sheets of white tagboard—one for each student. Make a sample doorknob hanger.

Instruct each student in the following procedures:

- Use scissors to cut out doorknob hanger.
- Letter one of the following messages on hanger: "Gonna catsup on my sleeping," "Orange you going to knock?" or "If you carrot all, come in."
- Illustrate message by using felt pens to draw a catsup bottle, an orange or a carrot.
- Trace glue over the letters and apply yarn.

Conversation Suggestions: **Do you feel angry when someone comes into your room without knocking? What makes you angry when you're at home? What do you do when you get angry? How might you respond in a loving way when you get angry?**

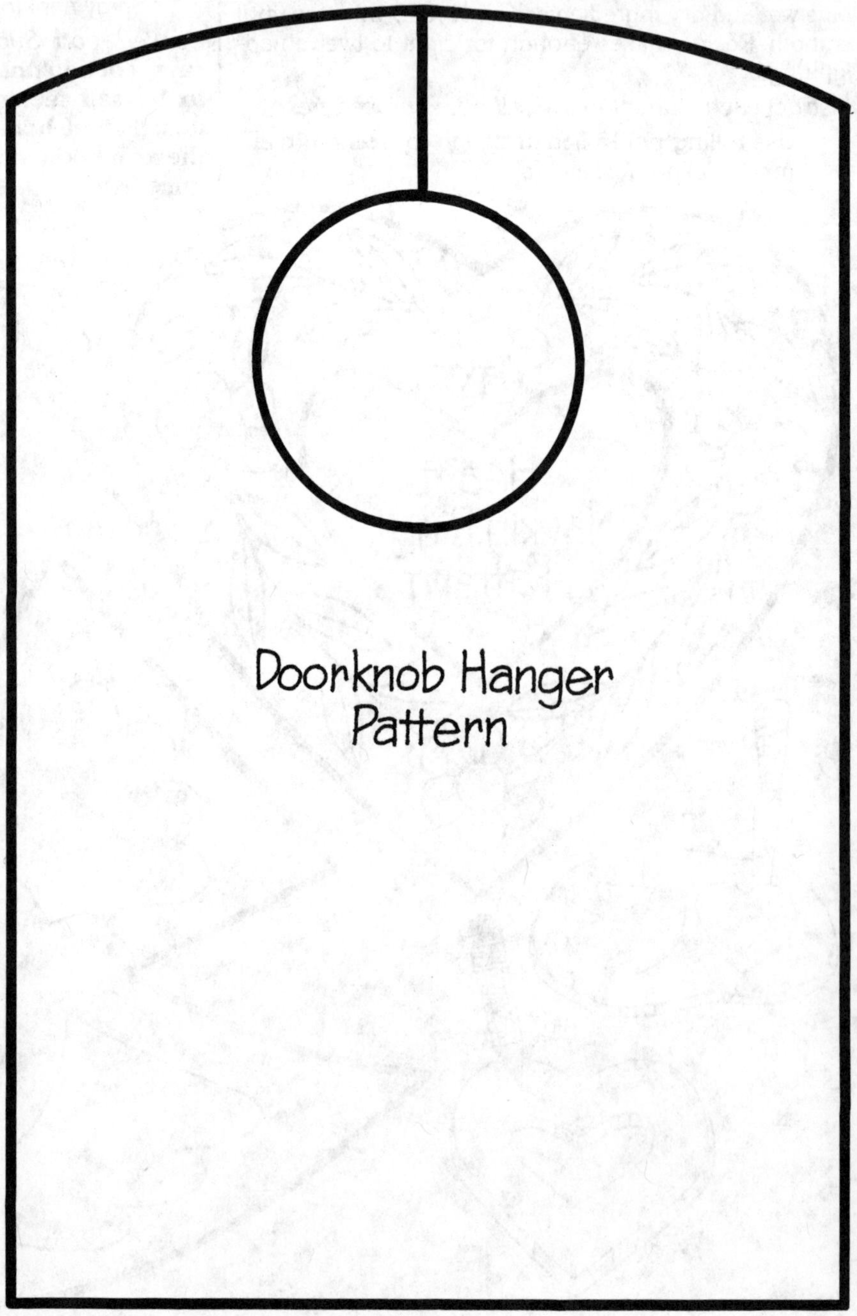

Swirl Banner

Materials: Shelf paper, large shallow pans, water, bright-colored oil paints, turpentine, small jars or bowls, clothespins, spoons, crayons, dowels, saw, glue, yarn, scissors.

Preparation: Cut shelf paper into 12-inch (30-cm) lengths. Mix turpentine with each color of oil paint until it is thin enough to pour. Put a small amount of water in each shallow pan. Cut dowels into 14-inch (35-cm) lengths—two for each student. Cut yarn into 24-inch (60-cm) lengths—one for each student.

Instruct each student in the following procedures:

- Use crayons to letter a simple slogan or draw a design on shelf paper. Crayon should be pressed firmly to get strong, bold colors.
- Pour a small amount of paint/turpentine mixture into water in pan. Stir slightly.
- Clip a clothespin to shelf paper to use as a handle.
- Gently lay paper facedown on water for a few seconds, allowing paint swirls to adhere to paper (see sketch). Paper can be moved back and forth to create variations with paint.
- Remove paper from water. Allow to dry.
- Glue dowels to top and bottom of paper.
- Tie yarn to top dowel for hanging.

Conversation Suggestions: **When is it difficult for children your age to tell the truth? Jesus told the truth even when those around Him told lies. This banner can help you remember to tell the truth.**

Sonrise Flower Pot

Materials: Enamel or acrylic paint, paintbrushes, paint thinner, newspapers, potting soil, hand shovels, newspapers, sunflower or marigold seeds or small potting plants. For each student—a small clay flower pot.

Preparation: Spread newspapers to cover work surface.

Instruct each student in the following procedures:

- Paint a design or message on the flower pot. Let dry.
- Fill pot with soil.
- Plant seeds or potting plant. Water lightly.

Conversation Suggestions: **Have you ever seen the sun rise or set? That is something we can count on to happen every day—no matter what. What else can you count on? We can *always* count on God. He is with us, loving us all the time—no matter what.**

Plaster Plaque

(One- or Two-Day Project)

Materials: Plaster of paris (approximately 1 lb. for each child), coffee cans, paint stirring sticks, sand, baking pans or foil-lined boxes, paper clips, water, measuring cup, spoons, pencils, assorted shells and pebbles, newspapers, clear acrylic spray. Optional—poster paints, paintbrushes, poster board, glue, scissors, felt pens.

Preparation: Place 2 to 3 inches (5 to 7.5 cm) of sand in pans or foil-lined boxes, one for each student. Wet sand just enough so it will hold shape. Cover work area with newspapers (or work outside).

Instruct each student in the following procedures:

- Level and smooth sand. Form a mold for plaque by making indentations in sand, at least ½ inch (1.25 cm) deep. Use hands, a spoon and pencil to form a design (sketch a).
- Press shells and pebbles into sand.
- Teacher assists students in preparing plaster according to package directions. Mix plaster and water in coffee cans, using paint stirring sticks.
- Quickly pour plaster into sand molds, filling indentations completely.
- Open up a paper clip part way (sketch b) and press it into wet plaster for hanger (sketch c).
- After a few minutes, when plaster has set, use another paper clip to scratch initials on plaque.
- Allow to dry overnight.
- The following day, remove plaque from sand and brush off excess sand.

Enrichment Idea: On second day, student decorates plaque with poster paints. After paint has dried, spray with clear acrylic spray. Student may cut shape from poster board, letter "God loves me" on shape and glue to plaque (see sketch).

Conversation Suggestions: **What is one reason we give gifts to people?** (To show we love them.) **What are some gifts God has given us to show He loves us? How will your plaque remind you of God's love?**

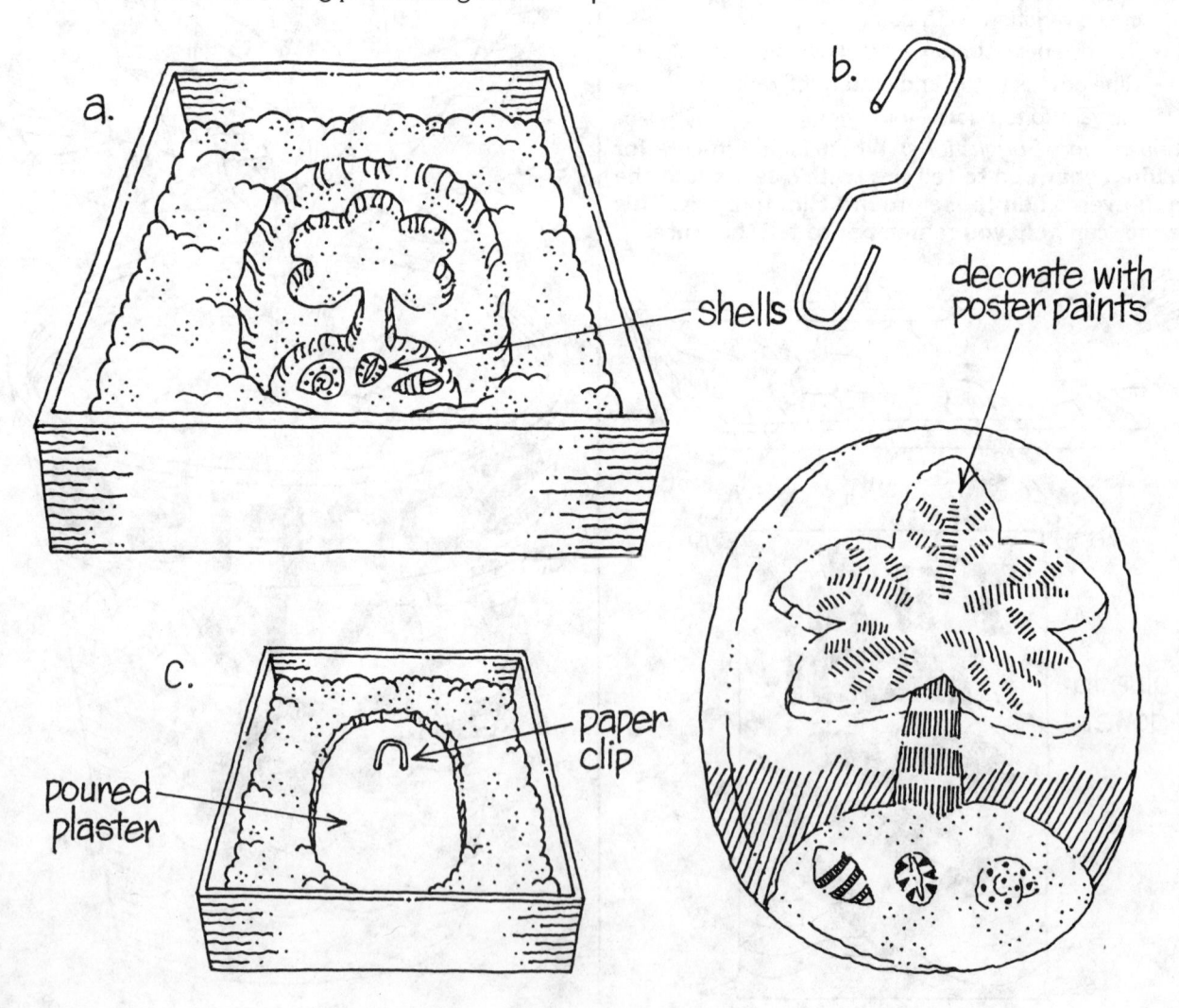

Tropical Fish Yarn Design

Materials: Variety of bright-colored yarn, 1/2-inch (1.25-cm) plywood, ruler, saw, sandpaper, white paint, paintbrushes, nails, hammers, pencils, picture-hangers, scissors. (Optional—large sequins.)

Preparation: Cut plywood into 8 × 10-inch (20 × 25-cm) pieces—one for each student. Sand wood pieces and paint them white. Let dry.

Instruct each student in the following procedures:

- Lightly draw outline of fish on wood (see sketch).
- Along outline of fish, about every inch, hammer nails halfway into wood.
- Hammer several more nails inside the outline for the eye, the fin and the mouth.
- Wind yarn around each nail, following shape of fish.
- Make eye, fin and mouth by winding yarn around nails inside fish outline. (Optional—thread sequins on yarn used to decorate inside of fish.)
- Attach picture hanger to top of wood.

Conversation Suggestions: **Why do you think it's important for people in God's family to show God's love through actions? What are some ways you might show God's love as we are working on our tropical fish?**

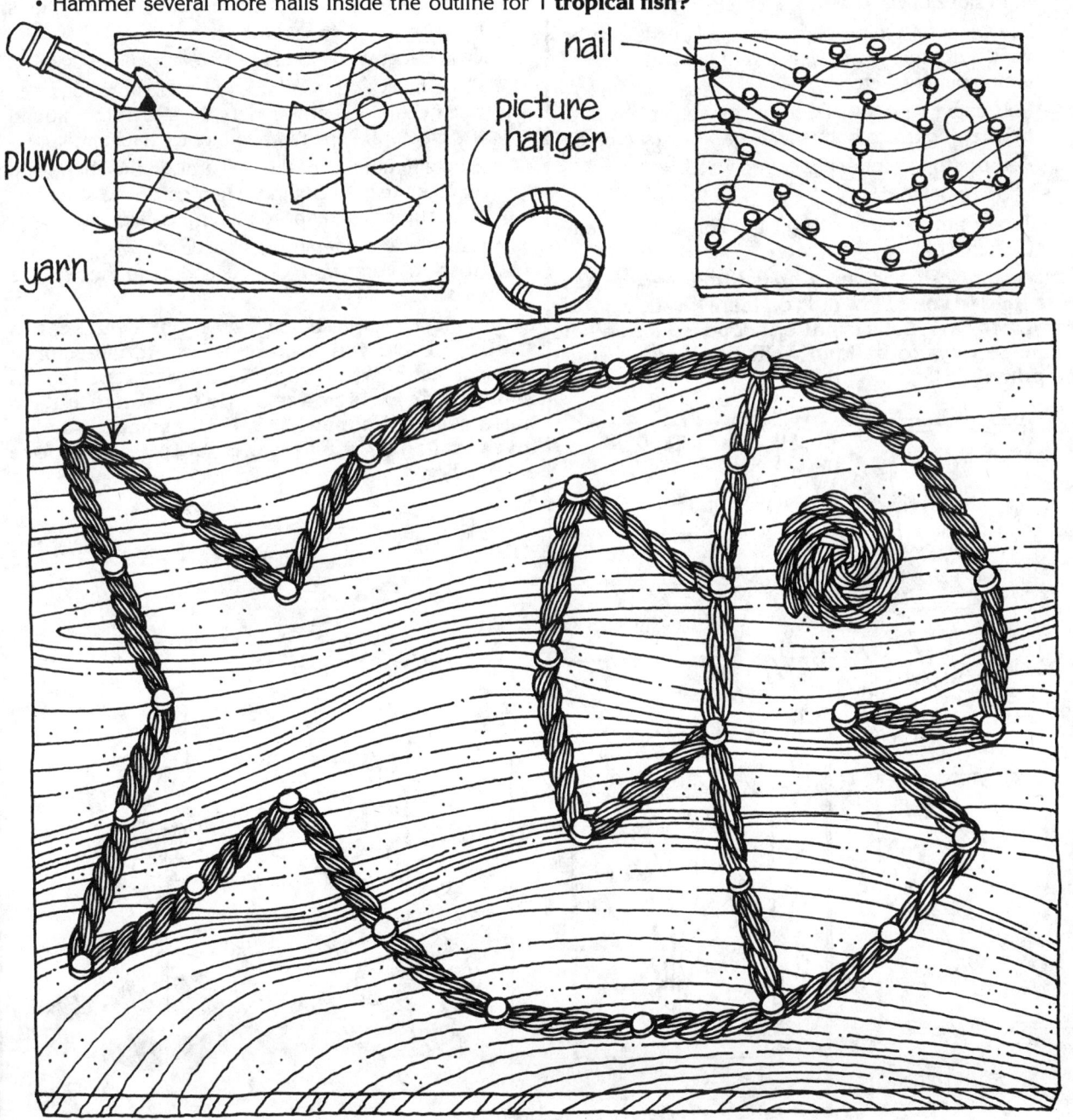

Mirror Ink Prints

Materials: Green weeds or tall grasses, typing paper, construction paper, tube of black water soluble printer's ink, 4-inch (10-cm) brayer (ink roller available at art supply store), cookie sheets, newspaper, tape.

Preparation: Cut an inside rectangle from each sheet of construction paper to make matting (sketch d). Cut one matte for each child. Cover table with newspaper.

Instruct each student in the following procedures:

- Squeeze 1 tsp. of ink on cookie sheet.
- Roll brayer in ink until brayer is evenly coated.
- Lay weed on another cookie sheet and roll ink onto both sides of weed with brayer (sketch a).
- Lay weed on typing paper. Several weeds can be used if desired. Cover weeds with another sheet of typing paper (sketch b).
- Rub paper with fingers, from the center outward, transferring ink to both sheets of paper (sketch c).
- Remove top sheet of paper and weed.
- Allow prints to dry.
- Tape print to back of construction paper matte (sketch d).

Conversation Suggestions: **Who is someone who has been kind to you? How did you feel? First Corinthians 13:4a says,** *Love is patient, love is kind.* **What are some ways to be kind while working on your ink prints?**

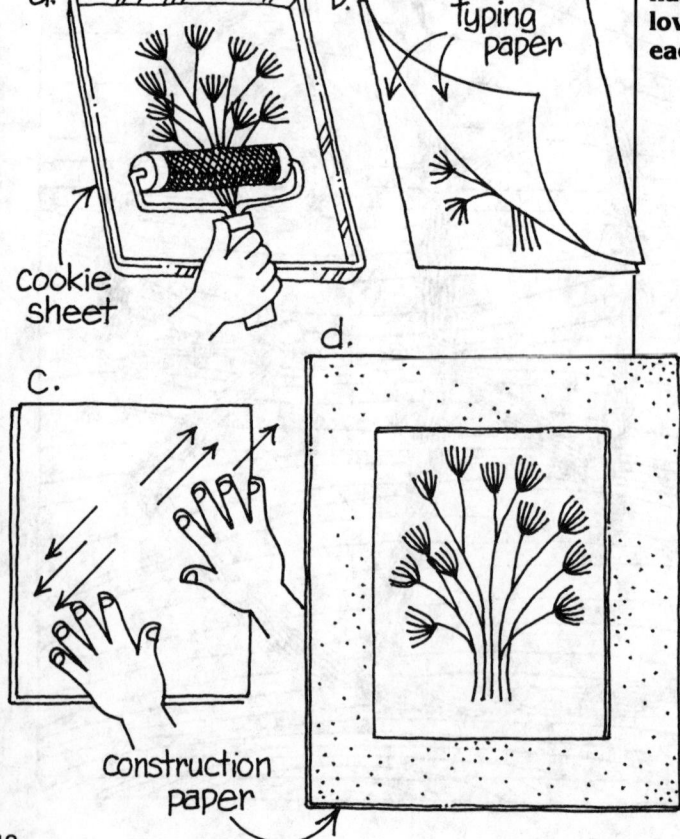

Underwater Mobile

Materials: Various light colors of felt, ¼-inch (6.25-mm) wooden dowels, ruler, saw, 4-strand embroidery floss, black carpet thread, polyester fiberfill stuffing, fabric glue, embroidery needles, scissors, pencils, lightweight cardboard.

Preparation: Cut dowels into 12-inch (30-cm) lengths—two for each student. Use patterns provided to make several cardboard patterns for students.

Instruct each student in the following procedures:

- Trace around cardboard patterns onto felt and cut out two of each shape.
- From contrasting colors of felt, cut out decorations for creatures (see sketch).
- Glue decorations to cut-out creatures. Let dry.
- Place back and front sides of a creature together. Use needle and embroidery floss to stitch around the creature. Repeat procedure for each creature.
- Stop stitching ¾ of the way around the shape and fill creature with stuffing. Then complete stitching. Repeat procedure for remaining creatures.
- Use black carpet thread to tie dowels together, hang creatures from dowels and hang mobile (see sketch).

Conversation Suggestions: **Have you ever seen a starfish? Have you ever seen beautifully-colored tropical fish? What does God's creation tell us about God? He is powerful, He is creative and He has a sense of humor! This is the same God who loves you and me and wants us to learn to love each other.**

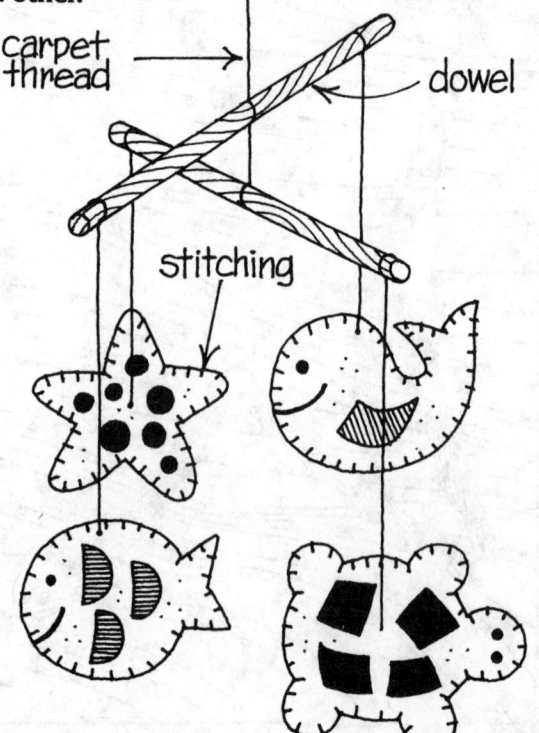

Underwater Mobile Patterns

Seaside Bath Delight

(Two-Day Project)
For Container:

Materials: Assortment of small seashells and stones, large bowl, small bowl, wooden spoon, flour (NOT self-rising), cornstarch, salt, glycerin, 1 cup water, plastic bag, rolling pins, cookie sheets, acrylic spray, oven. For each child—medium-size jar with metal lid.

Preparation: Make dough using the following recipe: Combine 2 cups flour, 1 cup cornstarch and 1 cup salt in large bowl. In small bowl mix 1 tsp. glycerin and 1 cup water. Combine wet and dry ingredients. Knead for 5 minutes until smooth. Place dough in plastic bag. Store dough in refrigerator overnight.

Instruct each student in the following procedures:

- Use rolling pin to flatten ball of dough into circle large enough to cover jar lid (sketch a).
- Mold dough around metal lid (sketch b).
- Press shells and stones into dough (sketch c).
- Place lid on cookie sheet and bake in oven at 275 degrees Fahrenheit (135 degrees Celcius) for one hour. Turn oven off and allow lid to cool in oven for one hour to eliminate cracking.
- Spray lid with acrylic spray.

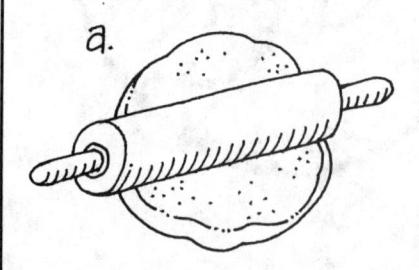

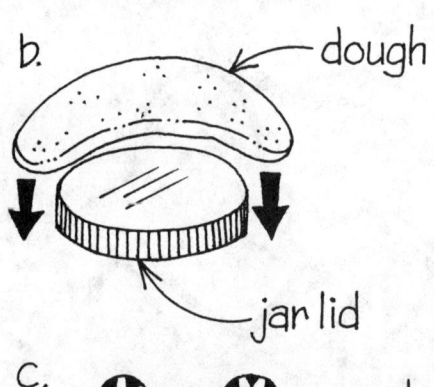

For Bath Oil:

Materials: Castile or baby shampoo, mineral oil or safflower oil, lemon flavor extract, wooden spoons, funnels, measuring cups and spoons, large sheet of paper, felt pen, tape, small index cards, pens, ribbon, scissors, hole punch.

Preparation: Cut ribbon into 18-inch (45-cm) lengths—one for each student. Letter the following directions on large sheet of paper. Tape to wall. DIRECTIONS: Shake well, pour ¼-cup under running water in tub, jump in and relax!

Instruct each student in the following procedures:

- Measure 1 cup shampoo and pour into jar.
- Measure ⅛ cup oil and pour into jar.
- Measure 1 tsp. lemon extract and pour into jar.
- Mix ingredients with wooden spoon.
- Screw lid tightly onto jar.
- Copy directions onto index card.
- Punch hole in card and put ribbon through hole.
- Tie ribbon around neck of jar.

Conversation Suggestions: **When is a time someone showed love to you?** Allow students to share examples. **Who is someone to whom you can show love in a special way this week? One way you might show love is by giving your Seaside Bath Delight as a gift!**

Huggy Panda Pencil

Materials: Black felt scraps, white glue, scissors. For each student—two white 1½-inch (3.75-cm) pom-poms, four black ½-inch (1.25-cm) pom-poms, seven ¼-inch (6.25-mm) pom-poms, two 7-mm wiggle eyes, new pencil.

Instruct each student in the following procedures:
- Glue the two white pom-poms together to form body and head.
- Glue one large black pom-pom to one small black pom-pom to form leg. Repeat three times to form other leg and arms.
- Glue small black pom-pom to front of head for nose.
- Glue two small black pom-poms to head for ears.
- Cut two small circles from black felt and glue to head for eyes.
- Glue wiggle eyes onto felt circles.
- Wrap paws around pencil and glue (see sketch).

Conversation Suggestions: **What does it mean to be generous? God has been generous to us—He sent His Son, Jesus, to show His love for us. What is a way you could be generous with your Panda Pencil?**

Linoleum Mosaic

(Two-Day Project)

Materials: Various colors of linoleum scraps (or textured wallpaper scraps), plywood, white glue, paper, pencils, grout, strong scissors or vinyl cutting tool, saw, damp cloth.

Preparation: Cut linoleum scraps or wallpaper into small "tiles." Cut plywood into 6-inch (15-cm) squares—one for each student.

Instruct each student in the following procedures:
- Use paper and pencil to make a simple sketch reflecting a Bible verse or story.
- Copy sketch onto plywood square.
- Glue linoleum (or wallpaper) tiles onto plywood to fit design (sketch a). (Some tiles may need to be trimmed as this is done.) Let dry.
- Fill spaces between tiles with grout. Then wipe tiles with damp cloth (sketch b).

Conversation Suggestions: **What is the most important thing you learned in our lesson today? What design can you make on your mosaic that will remind you of what you learned?**

Bird Feeder

Materials: Half-gallon milk carton for each student, poster board, scissors, pencils, crayons or felt pens, clear self-adhesive plastic, stapler and staples, awl or ice pick, string, wooden dowels, bird seed, craft knife.

Preparation: For each student: Cut poster board and self-adhesive plastic to cover top of milk cartons. Cut a portion out of one side of each milk carton (sketch a). Cut dowels into 8-inch (20-cm) lengths—one for each student. Cut string into 24-inch (60-cm) lengths—one for each student.

Instruct each student in the following procedures:

- Use crayons or felt pens to decorate poster board piece with design, verse or message (sketch b).
- Cover the poster board piece with self-adhesive plastic.
- Bend poster board in half and staple to top of milk carton for roof (sketch c).
- Use awl or ice pick to punch holes in opposite sides of milk carton as shown in sketch d.
- Thread string through holes and tie in knot for hanger (sketch d).
- Punch holes in opposite sides of bottom of milk carton, enlarge holes with a pencil and insert dowel (sketch e).
- Fill bottom of bird house with bird seed.

Conversation Suggestions: **What do baby birds need to be healthy and to grow?** (Food, water, safe nest, freedom to fly, etc.) **What do we need to help us grow as God's children?** (The Bible, prayer, Christian teachers and friends.)

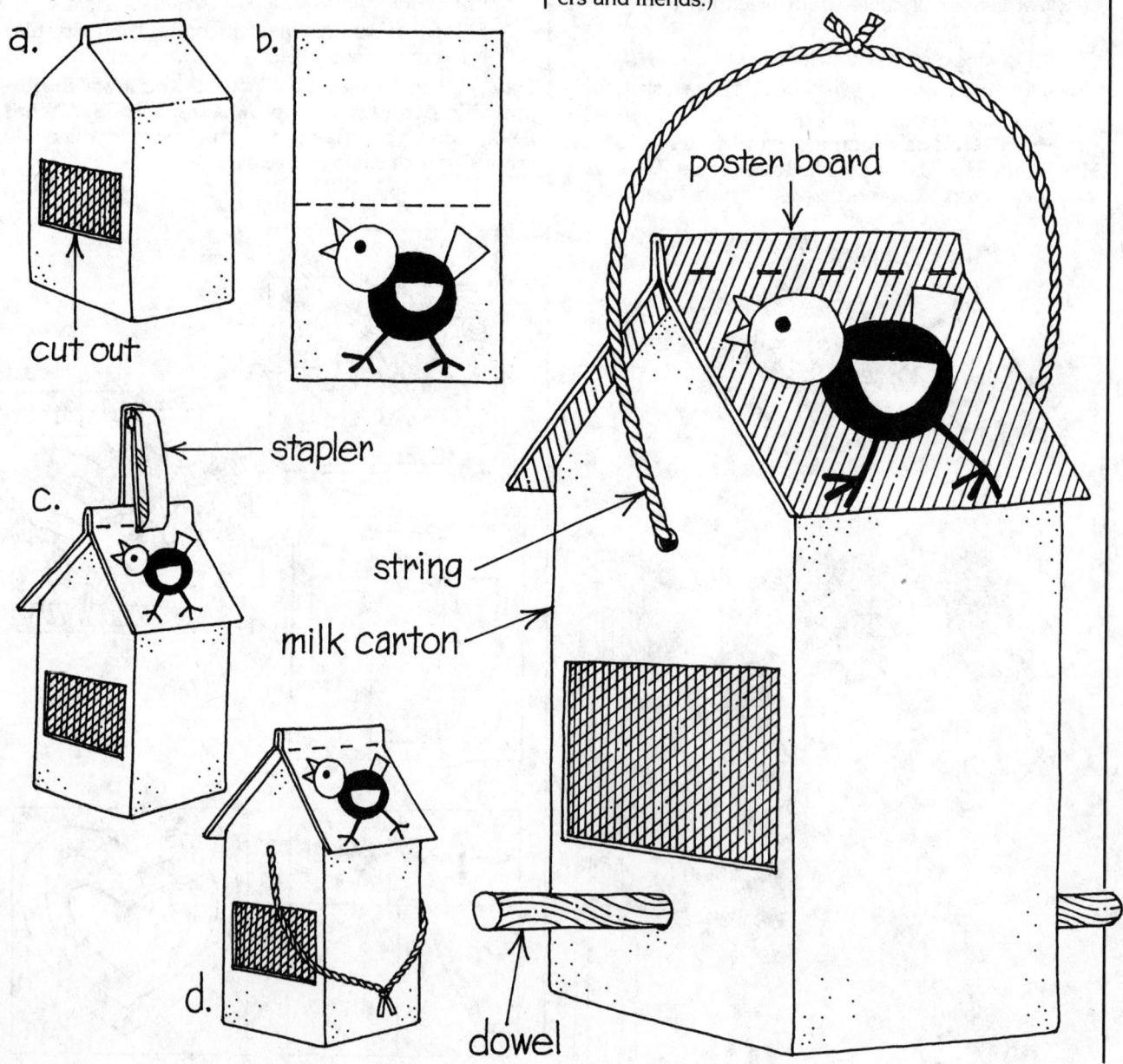

Wire Bracelet

Materials: Dove, Heart, and Fish Patterns, lightweight cardboard, pencil, scissors, 20-gauge copper or aluminum or galvanized wire (available from hobby, hardware or radio repair shops), ruler, tin cans or jars approximately 9-inches (22.5-cm) in circumference, needle-nosed pliers.

Preparation: Trace Patterns onto cardboard to make one of each pattern for every two to three students. (See "How to Make Patterns," p. 9.) Cut wire into 40-inch (100-cm) lengths for bracelet—one for each student. Cut wire into 10-inch (25-cm) lengths for charms—one for each student.

Instruct each student in the following procedures:

- Wrap one end of longer wire around can, leaving one short end and one long end (sketch a).
- Carefully remove wire circle from can and wrap the short end of free wire around circle to secure (sketch b).
- Twist remaining wire around circle making smooth, even twists (sketch c). Continue around circle several times until all wire has been used (sketch d). Use pliers to carefully hide the end of wire among the twists.
- Lay shorter length of wire on charm pattern and bend wire to match shape.
- Place charm on bracelet and use pliers to twist ends of charm together (sketch e).

Conversation Suggestions: **Are you proud of what you made? I'm glad you like what you made! What is a way you can express your pride without bragging?**

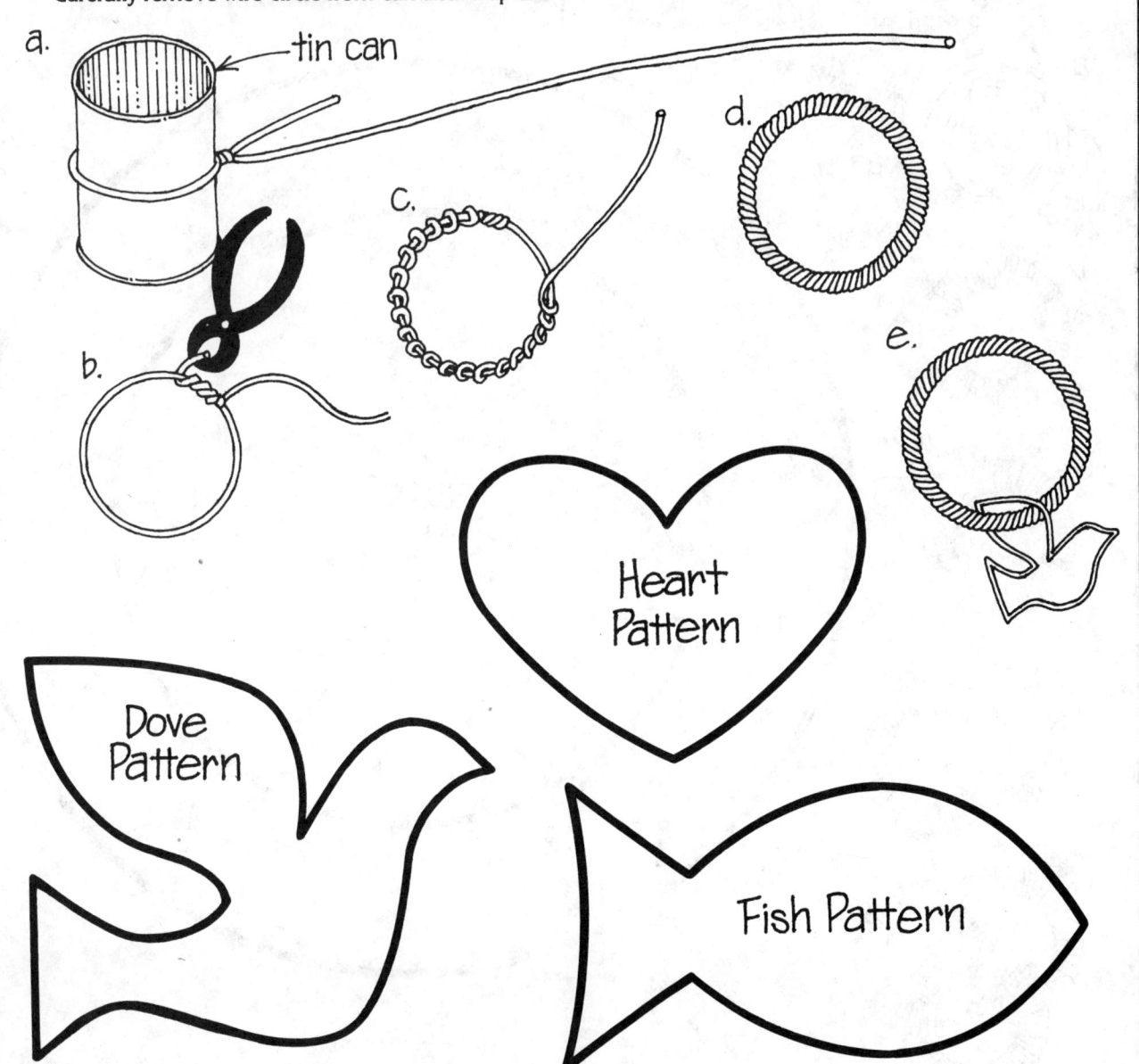

53

Trefoil (A Symbol of the Godhead)

Materials: Lightweight cardboard, three colors of yarn, pencils, scissors, glue, tape.

Preparation: Trace Trefoil Pattern onto cardboard and cut out. (See "How to Make Patterns," p. 9.) Make one pattern for every two to three children. Cut cardboard into 6 × 18-inch (15 × 45-cm) pieces—one for each student. Cut yarn into 7-yard (6.3-m) lengths—one of each color for each student.

Instruct each student in the following procedures:

- Use pattern to trace three circles onto cardboard and cut out.
- Draw a line of glue around one side of cardboard circle. Tape end of yarn to circle (sketch a).
- Wrap yarn around circle until entire circle is covered with yarn (sketch b). Glue end of yarn under yarn wrapping to secure.
- For the second circle, repeat the process, but leave 4-inches (10-cm) of cardboard uncovered.
- Cut apart the second circle in the uncovered area (sketch c).
- Join first and second circles and tape second circle to secure (sketch d).
- Continue wrapping yarn around second circle to finish.
- Repeat process for third circle. Third circle should be joined to first and second circles so the three are intertwined (sketch e).

Conversation Suggestions: **The three rings on your trefoil represent the three persons of God—the Father, the Son and the Holy Spirit. When did Jesus promise that God would send the Holy Spirit? How do you think that made the disciples feel? In what way is God with us today?**

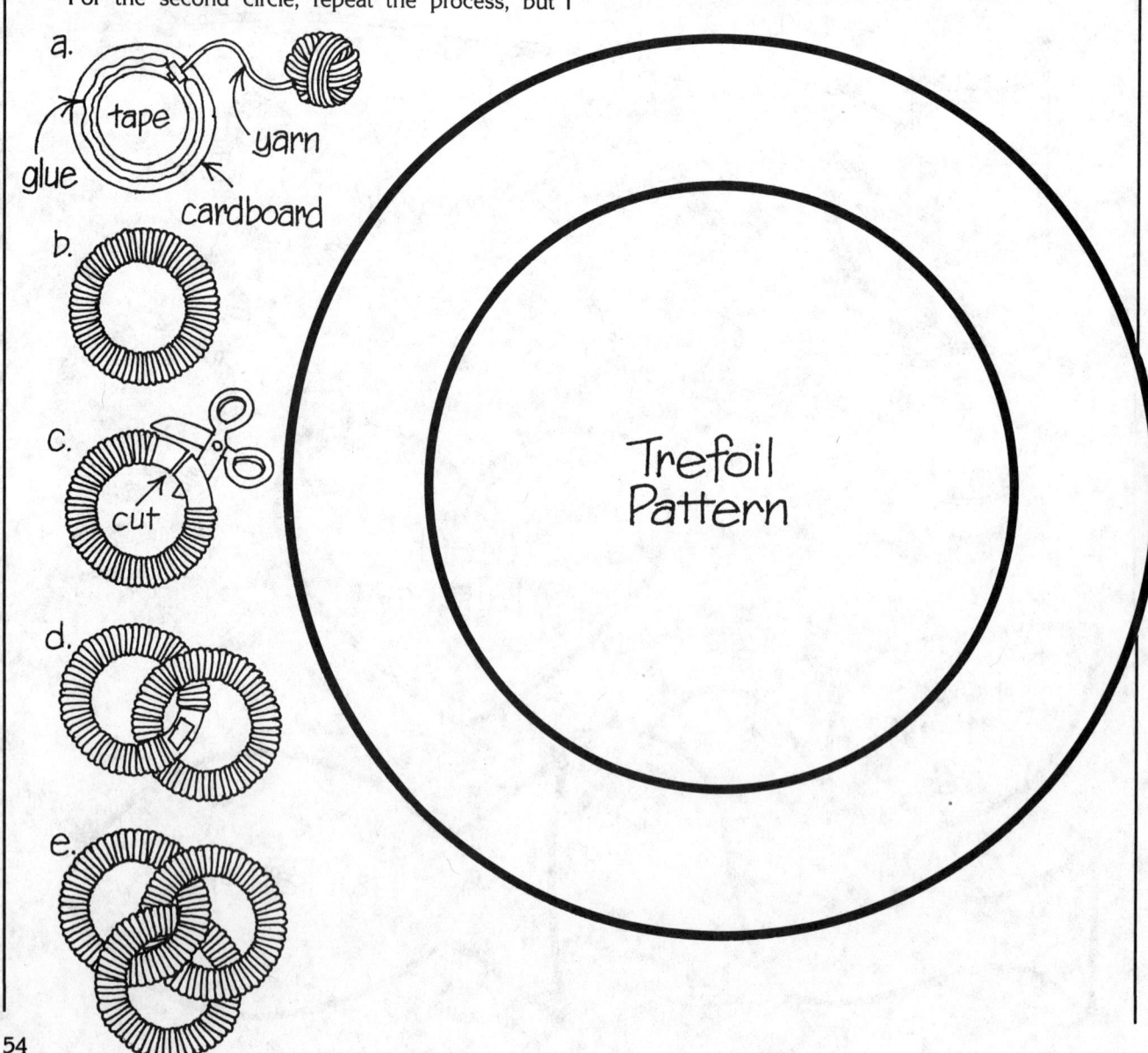

SECTION 4/GRADES 6-9

Crafts for Youth

Crafts can be exciting, fun ways to challenge youth to use or develop creative abilities. This section provides instructions for a variety of craft projects that will appeal to young people. Be sure to read the directions carefully and to gather materials or make other preparations well in advance.

When is the best time to do your crafts? It may be as students arrive (especially if they have a tendency to arrive late), or after the Bible study while students continue to talk about what they have learned from God's Word.

If you want to relate a craft project to the specific lesson you're teaching, suggest specific designs where appropriate. For example, students making wooden notebooks may design a journal for keeping Bible study notes, or for recording thoughts on a particular topic. The lesson's Bible verse may be lettered on some of the crafts. You can also take the opportunity to point out specific ways students are modeling Christian character qualities or showing signs of spiritual growth and maturity.

Working together on craft projects provides many opportunities for cooperation and encouragement. You'll find that Christian growth concepts can easily be reinforced as you comment on your students' attitudes and actions.

Cigar Box Collage

Materials: Scissors, glue, clear acrylic spray, picture hangers, felt pens, scraps of wallpaper, fabric, ribbon, lace, a variety of items brought in by students (such as: candy wrappers, photographs, magazine pictures, buttons, old keys, small figures, postcards, coins). For each student—one cigar box.

Instruct each student in the following procedures:

- Choose pictures and items that reflect a theme (such as: All About Me; Island Living; Growing Up; Sports).
- Line inside of cigar box and lid with wallpaper or fabric scraps.
- Arrange photographs and items in cigar box and inside lid.
- Glue items in place and let dry.
- Spray collage with clear acrylic spray.
- Attach picture hanger to back of box so that when box is hung on wall, lid hinge will be at bottom of box.

Landscape in a Basket

Materials: Sheets of plastic cut from an inexpensive dropcloth, potting soil, activated charcoal (available at nursery), water, scissors, assorted nature items (driftwood, twigs, pebbles, small rocks, pinecones, shells, etc.). For each student—two or three 2-inch (5-cm) plants; wide, shallow basket of any type.

Instruct each student in the following procedures:

- Line basket with plastic so that the plastic drapes over edges of basket (sketch a).
- Fill bottom of basket with 1/4-inch (.6-cm) layer of charcoal.
- Add potting soil to just below rim of basket. Press gently.
- Dig holes for plants.
- Put plants in holes and pat soil firmly.
- Add nature items for decoration. A small twig or driftwood looks like a fallen tree. Sand and pebbles make a beach.
- Trim off excess plastic with scissors.
- Keep garden where it gets lots of light, but don't put in direct sunlight or parts of the plant may burn. Water when the top inch of soil dries out.

56

"Stone" Carving

Materials: Plastic bucket, large mixing spoon, agricultural vermiculite (found in garden supply stores), plaster of paris, patching cement (found in hardware stores), water, white glue, clear acrylic spray, measuring cups. For each student—a 1-pint milk carton, paring or pocket knife, pencil, tracing paper, piece of medium-fine sand paper, sheet of carbon paper.

Preparation: Cut tops off 1-pint milk cartons—one for each student (sketch a). In bucket, mix 6 cups vermiculite, 6 cups plaster of paris and 3 cups patching cement. As you stir, slowly add enough water to make a thick, creamy texture. Pour mixture into milk cartons. (Recipe should fill 4 cartons.) Rinse tools out-of-doors as mixture may clog drain pipes. Allow two days for mixture to harden.

Instruct each student in the following procedures:

- Tear milk carton away from hardened block.
- Use tracing paper and pencil to sketch a simple design to carve.
- Place carbon paper between tracing paper and block and re-trace the pattern so it shows up on block (sketch b). Turn paper over and repeat on other side of block.
- Use pocket knife to cut into block, following the pattern. Make shallow cuts, gradually working deep enough to form the shape of pattern.
- Further shape the rough form by more detailed carving (sketch c).
- Use sandpaper to smooth the contours; however, don't expect to get fine details.
- Use glue to repair any broken pieces. Let dry.
- Spray with clear acrylic spray to help weatherproof and protect surface.

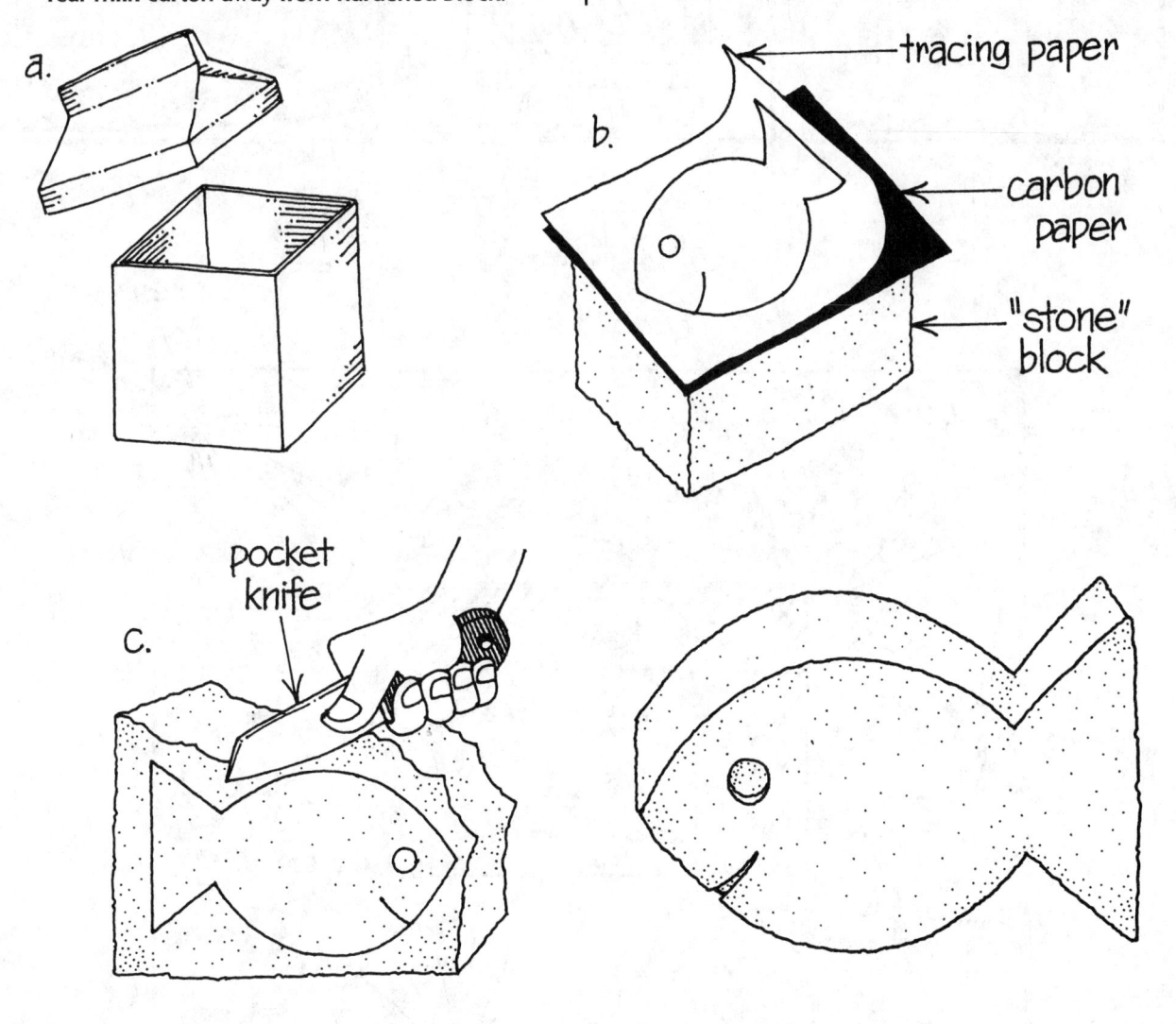

Seashell Picture Frame

Materials: Shells, scissors, craft knives, pencils, rulers, colored poster board, masking tape. For each student—a favorite photo (alert students in advance to bring a favorite photo to this session).

Instruct each student in the following procedures:

- Cut two pieces of poster board to the desired size and shape of a frame to fit his or her photo.
- Lightly trace around photo onto one of the pieces of poster board.
- Use ruler to draw smaller outline ¼-inch (.6-cm) inside original outline (sketch a).
- Use craft knife to cut out the smaller outline.
- Center photo behind cut-out area of frame.
- Tape photo to the back of frame (sketch b).
- Glue second piece of poster board to back of frame (sketch c).
- Arrange shells on front of frame and glue in place (sketch d).

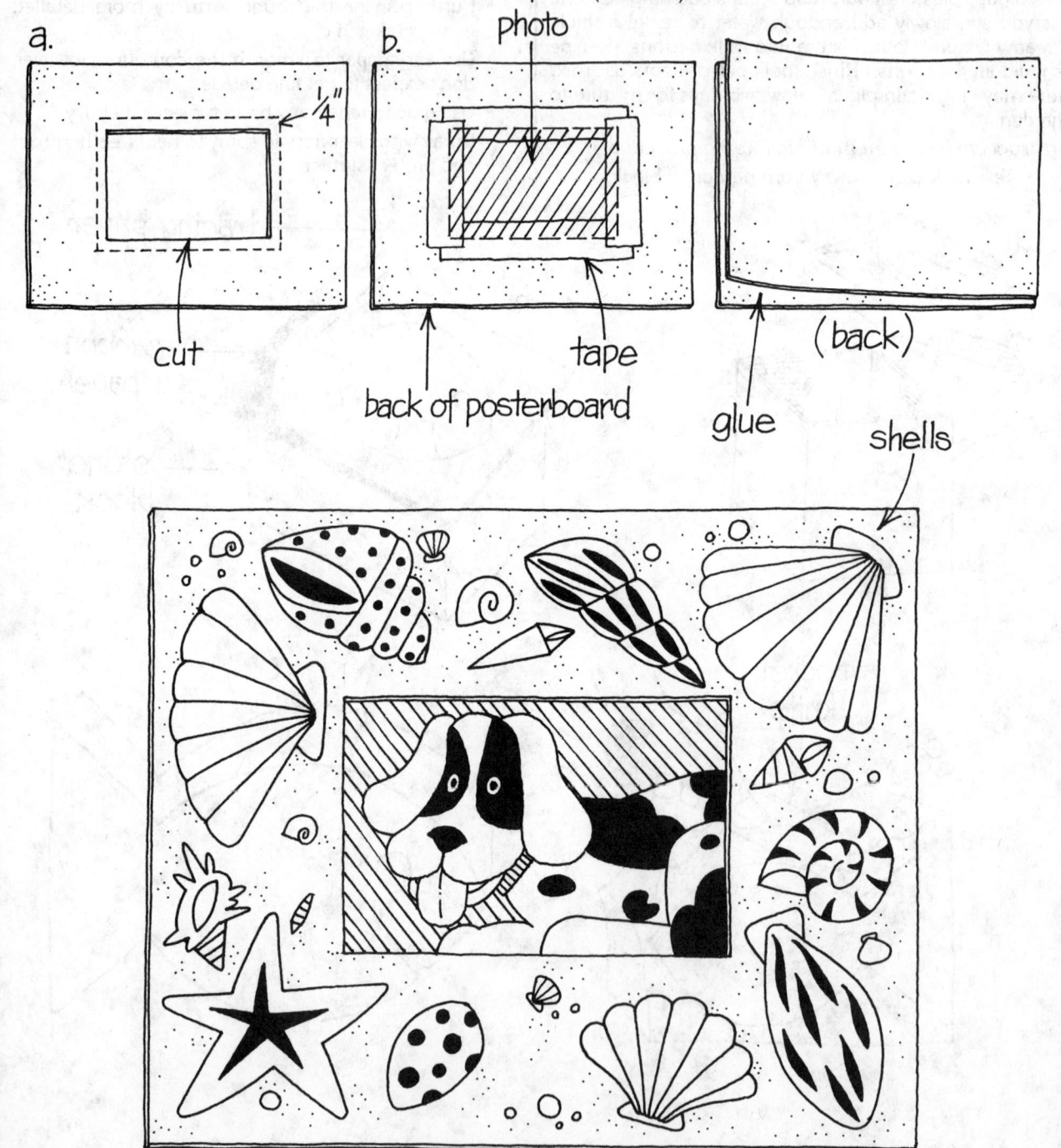

Decorative Wire Basket

Materials: Felt, scissors, pens, miniature fabric flowers (available at craft stores), assorted colors of ribbon and lace. For each student—small wire basket (available at craft stores).

Instruct each student in the following procedures:

- Weave lengths of ribbon and lace through wire basket (sketch a).
- Leave an equal length of ribbon at beginning and end of weaving (sketch b).
- Tie excess ribbon in a bow (sketch c).
- Attach fabric flowers to basket by winding the green wire on the flowers around the wire of basket (sketch d).
- Use pen to trace the bottom of basket onto felt. Cut out.
- Place the felt in the bottom of basket.

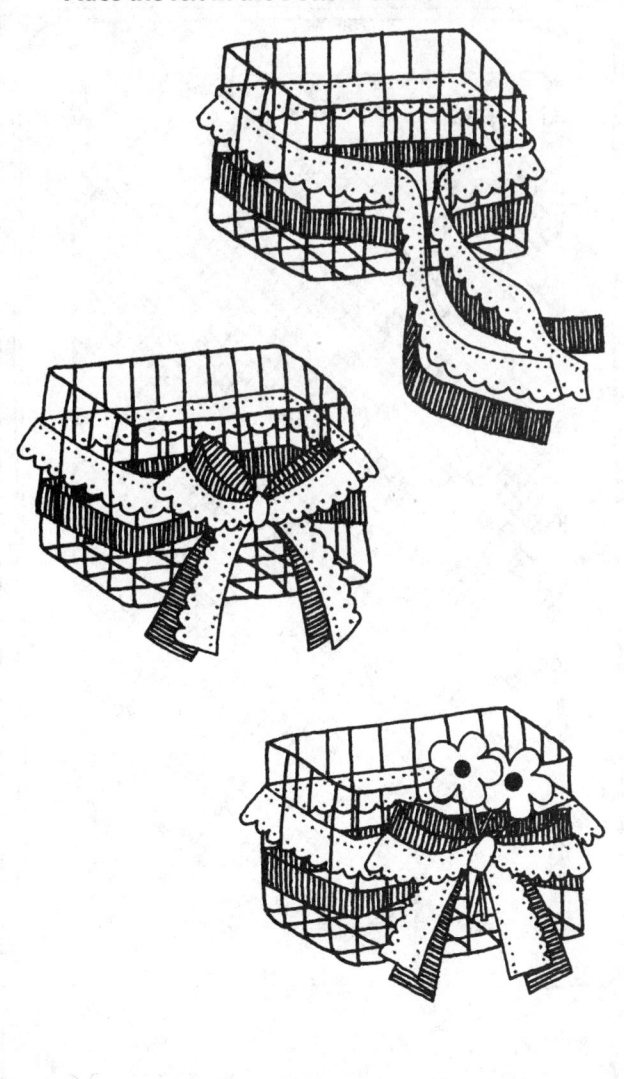

Tropical Fruit Magnets

Materials: Small paintbrushes, acrylic paints (in a variety of colors, including white), water, paper cups, clear acrylic spray. For each student—several plaster fruit magnets (available at statuary and craft stores).

Instruct each student in the following procedures:

- Paint the entire magnet with white acrylic paint. Let dry.
- Paint magnet desired colors. (Start by painting the largest section and finish by painting details.) Rinse brush thoroughly in cup of water before changing colors. Let magnet dry for several minutes.
- When dry, spray magnet with a thin coat of clear acrylic spray.
- Allow to dry for fifteen minutes before handling.

Shell Comb

Materials: Small shells, white glue or hot glue gun and glue sticks. For each student—comb. Optional—a large, plain barrette may be used in place of the comb.

Instruct each student in the following procedures:
- Cover with glue the entire band above the teeth of comb and allow to set for one or two minutes. (If you use a hot glue gun, do not allow to set. Glue on shells immediately.)
- Place shells in a design, pressing firmly into glue. Place some shells faceup and some facedown.
- Let glue dry thoroughly before use.
- Encourage boys to give their combs to female family member or friend.

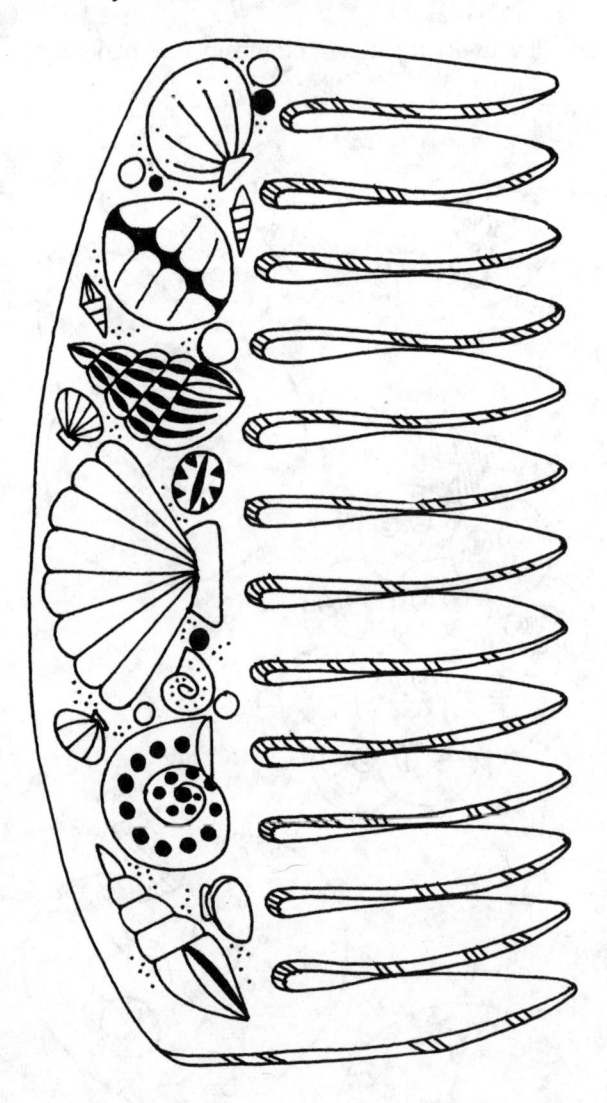

Personal Chalkboard

Materials: Various colors of acrylic paints, paintbrushes, paper cups, water, clear acrylic finish, hammer. For each student—a small chalkboard with wooden frame (available at craft stores) and a sawtooth picture hanger with nails.

Instruct each student in the following procedures:
- Paint frame of chalkboard. Using a very wet paintbrush will give the frame a "washed" look.
- Paint name and other designs directly on chalkboard (see sketch). Let dry.
- Use paintbrush to apply the clear finish to frame and painted areas on chalkboard. (Chalkboard will not be usable if entire surface is covered with finish.)
- Place picture hanger on back of frame and gently hammer nails in place.

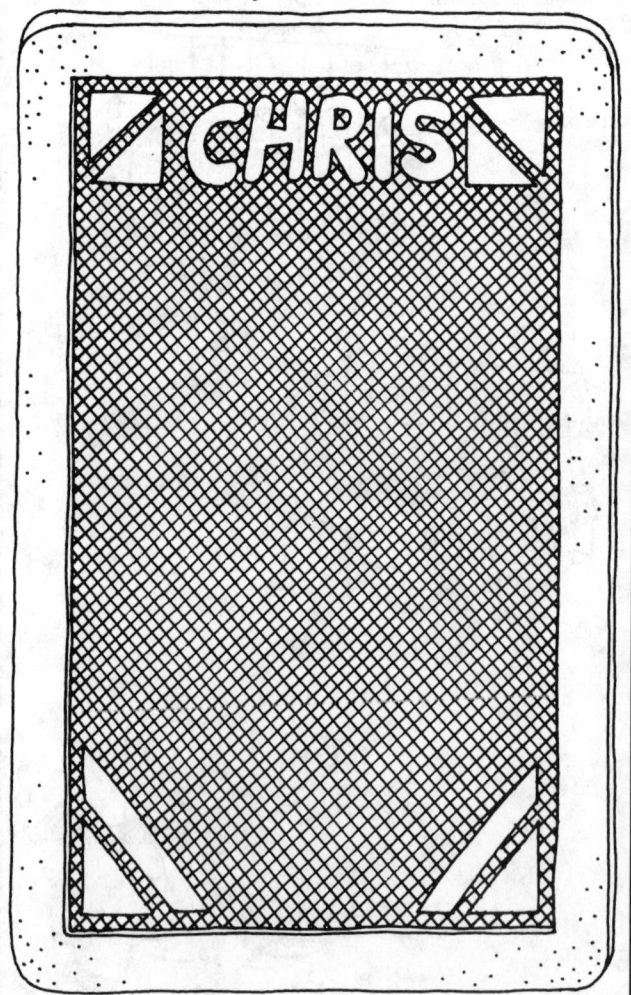

Friendship Bracelet

Materials: For each student—three 3-foot (.9-m) lengths of thin satin cord in assorted colors, three beads with holes large enough to slip over the three pieces of cord.

Instruct each student in the following procedures:
- Tie one end of each length of cord to the rung of a chair or to another sturdy object (sketch a).
- Knot cords approximately 3 inches (7.5-cm) from tied ends (sketch b).
- Slip one bead over cords (sketch c).
- Knot cords again on other side of bead (sketch d).
- Braid cord six times and knot (sketch e).
- Add another bead and knot cord again.
- Braid cord, knot, add bead and knot again.
- Cut cords approximately 3 inches (7.5-cm) from last knot.
- Untie cords from chair.
- Cut cords approximately 3 inches (7.5-cm) from first knot.

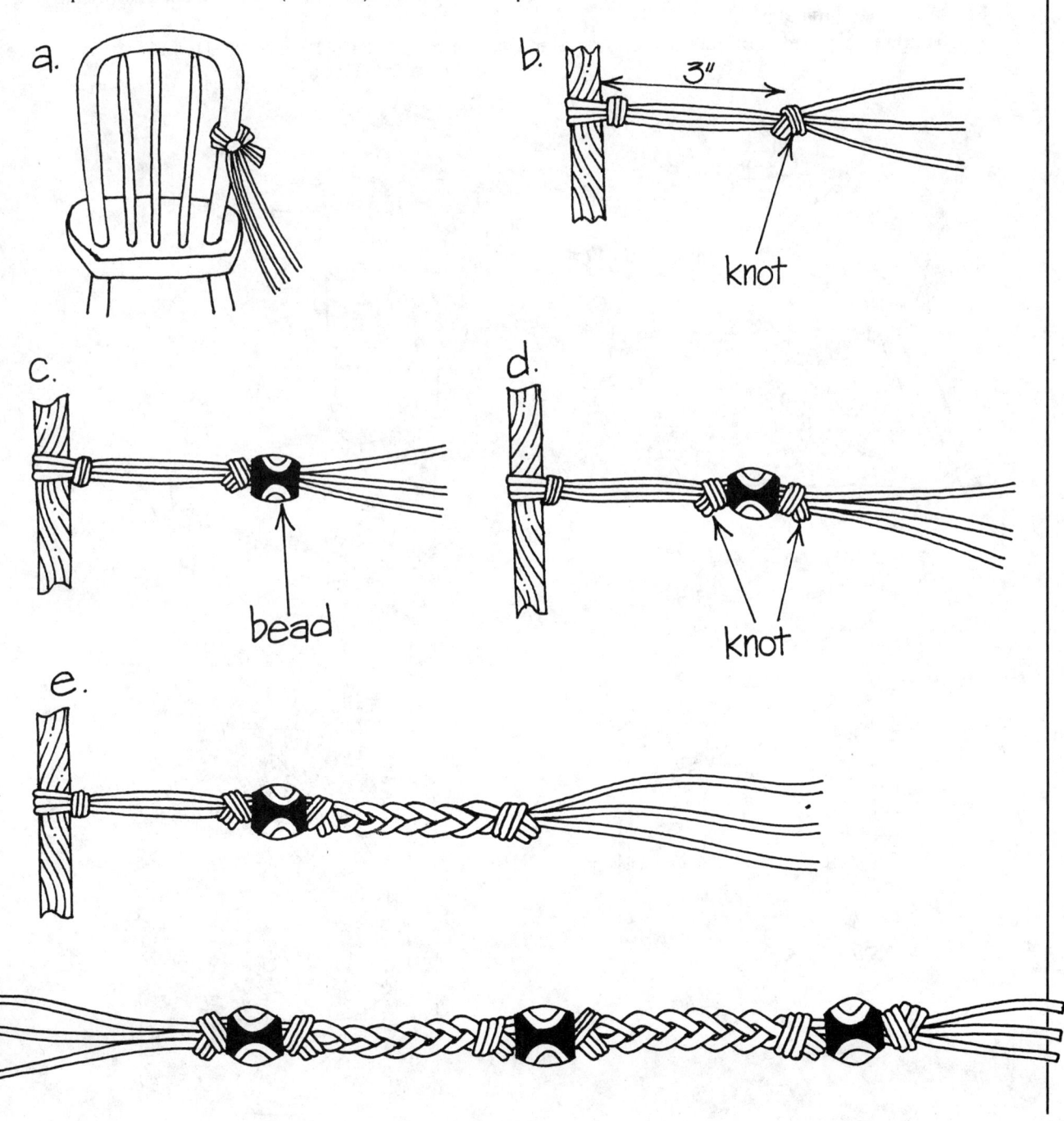

Rainbow Jar

Materials: Paper cups, white sand, water, food coloring, plastic spoons, paper towels, small shells. For each student—a small, decorative jar with a cork lid.

Instruct each student in the following procedures:

- Fill three or four paper cups half-full of sand.
- Add water to cover sand completely.
- Add a different color of food coloring to each cup of water and sand. (The more coloring you add, the deeper the color sand.)
- Stir sand, water and coloring with a plastic spoon. Let stand several minutes.
- Pinch edge of cup and pour out most of the water without losing sand. (Colored water may be poured into another student's cup of undyed sand.)
- Spoon sand from each cup onto separate sheets of paper towels.
- Spread out sand and let dry (sketch a).
- Spoon a layer of colored sand into jar (sketch b).
- Carefully spoon various layers of colored sand on top of one another into jar. The last layer should barely come to the neck of the jar (sketch c).
- Arrange shells on top of the sand, touching edge of jar (sketch d).
- Spoon in a last layer of sand to hold shells in place. Place cork lid on jar.

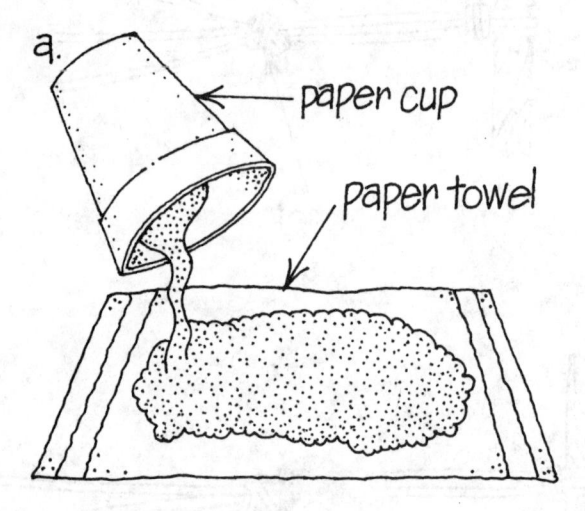

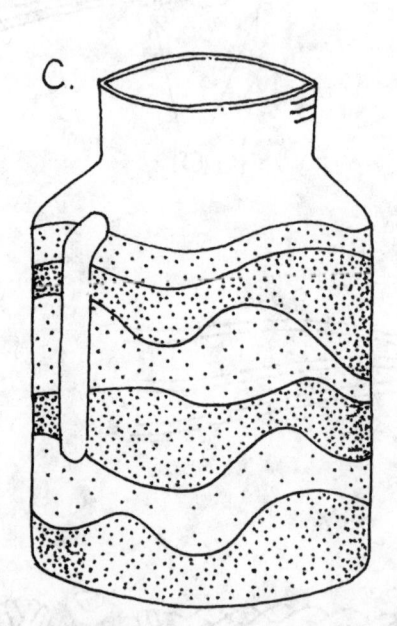

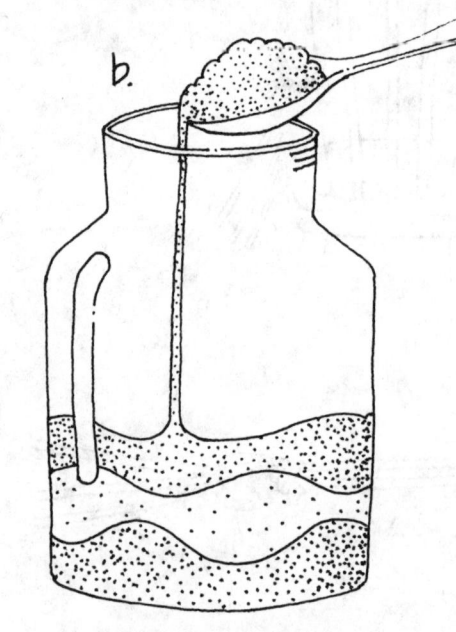

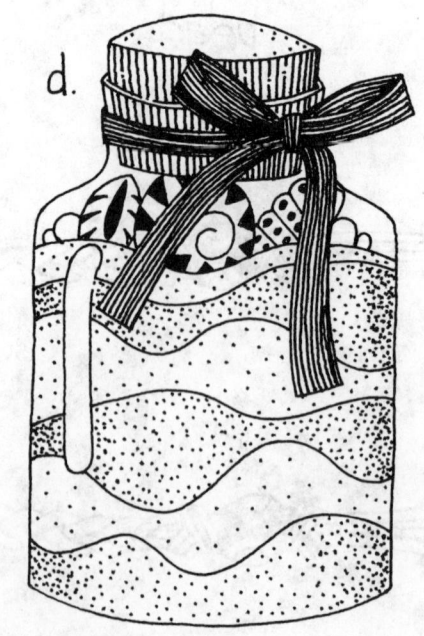

SECTION 5

Reproducible Pages

Bible Memory Verse Coloring Pages

The following pages are reproducible and contain ten Bible Memory Verse designs for younger elementary children and ten for older elementary children. Ideas for using these pages include:

1. Use the photocopied pages as rewards for children who memorize the Bible verse. They may take the page home to color and display.

2. Use the pages in class for transition times or for advanced students who finish an activity ahead of other students.

3. Play a coloring game. Place a variety of felt pens on the table. Recite the verse together. Then each student may choose a pen and use it to color on his or her page for one minute. When time is up, students put pens down and repeat verse together again. Students then choose another pen and color for one minute. Repeat process until pages are completed or students tire of activity.

4. To customize pages, cover the Bible verse with white paper and letter another verse or saying in its place before you photocopy.

Student Certificates and Awards

The awards and certificates on the following pages may be personalized for various uses. Just follow these simple procedures:

1. Tear out certificate and letter the name of your program on the appropriate line.

2. Photocopy as many copies of certificate as needed.

3. Letter each child's certificate with his or her name (and achievement when appropriate).

"This is how God showed his love among us: He sent his one and only Son into the world that we might live through him." 1 John 4:9

"If I speak... but have not love, I am only a resounding gong or a clanging cymbal." I Corinthians 13:1

GRADES 1-2 Coloring Page 2

"If I give all I possess to the poor...but have not love, I gain nothing." I Corinthians 13:3

"Love is patient, love is kind." I Corinthians 13:4a

GRADES 1-2 Coloring Page 4

"Love...does not envy." I Corinthians 13:4b

"Love... does not boast, it is not proud." I Corinthians 13:4b

GRADES 1-2 Coloring Page 6

"Love...is not rude, it is not self-seeking."
1 Corinthians 13:5

"Love...is not easily angered, it keeps no record of wrongs." 1 Corinthians 13:5b

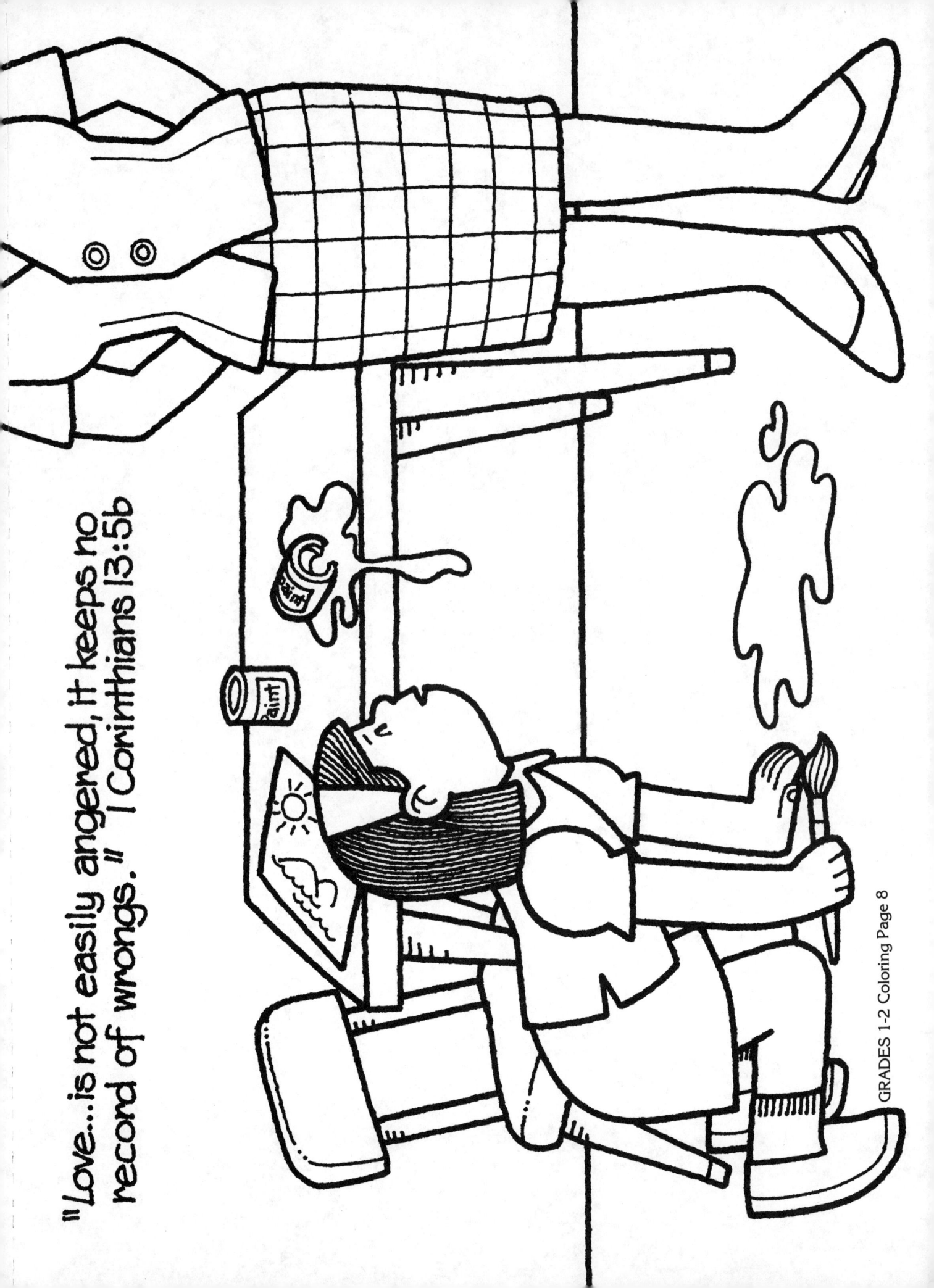

"Love does not delight in evil but rejoices with the truth." I Corinthians 13:6

Tell the truth

"Love...always protects, always trusts, always hopes, always perseveres."
I Corinthians 13:7

GRADES 1-2 Coloring Page 10

"This is how God showed his love among us: He sent his one and only Son into the world that we might live through him." 1 John 4:9

GRADES 3-6 Coloring Page 1

"If I speak...but have not love, I am only a resounding gong or a clanging cymbal." I Corinthians 13:1

"If I give all I possess to the poor...but have not love, I gain nothing." I Corinthians 13:3

"Love is patient, love is kind."
1 Corinthians 13:4a

"Love...does not envy."
1 Corinthians 13:4b

GRADES 3-6 Coloring Page 6

"Love...does not boast, it is not proud." I Corinthians 13:4b

"Love...is not rude, it is not self-seeking."
I Corinthians 13:5

"Love...is not easily angered, it keeps no record of wrongs."
1 Corinthians 13:5b

"Love does not delight in evil but rejoices with the truth." 1 Corinthians 13:6

"Love...always protects, always trusts, always hopes, always perseveres." I Corinthians 13:7

Attendance Award

presented to

_____

for attendance at

_____

| Place sticker here | Place sticker here | Place sticker here | Place sticker here | Place sticker here |

This is to certify that

memorized all the Bible Memory Verses at

Place sticker here

Place sticker here

Place sticker here

Place sticker here

Place sticker here

Happy Helper Award

_____

was a cheerful helper at

_____

Visitor Award

_____,

we're glad you came to

_____

_____

showed kindness today by

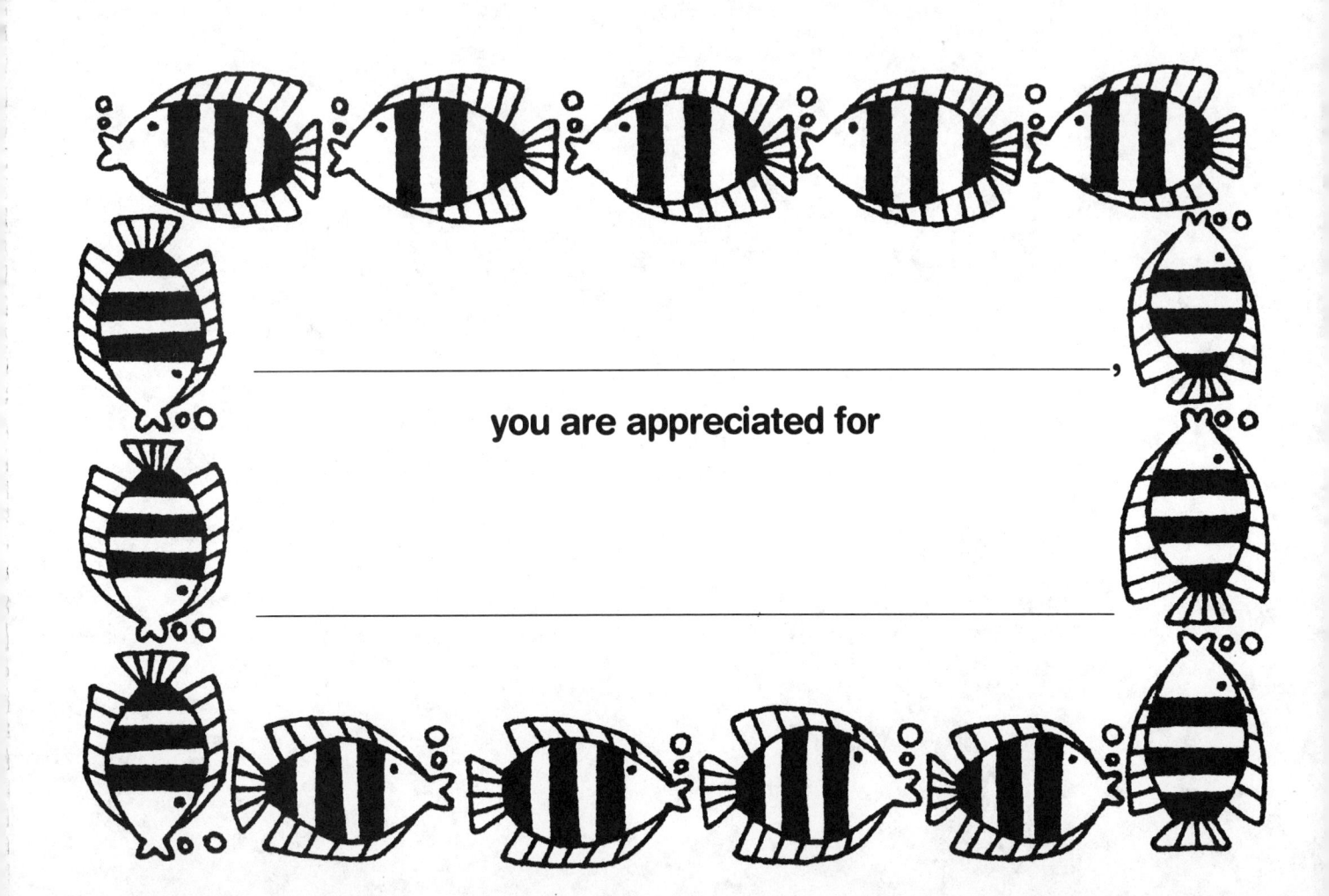

_____

_____, **you are appreciated for**

_____